Harry from Al.

The

ODYSSEUM

DAVID BRAMWELL
& JO TINSLEY

The

ODYSSEUM

DAVID BRAMWELL
& JO TINSLEY

ISBN 9781473668980
eISBN 9781473668966

Carmelite House
50 Victoria Embankment
London EC4Y 0DZ

www.chambers.co.uk

Also available
as an ebook

Editor: Jo Tinsley
Art director: Tina Smith
Designer: Johnathan Montelongo
Production: Dave Perrett
Research: Matthew Iredale, Guy Lochhead

Contents

Introduction

For a short while in the early 1980s Monty Python's Graham Chapman was a member of the notorious Dangerous Sports Club. In his occasional role as warm-up act for The Who, Chapman liked to recount hair-raising tales of how he and fellow members of the club travelled down ski slopes on hospital beds, wheelchairs and grand pianos, half joking that the last one to break a leg was the winner. Chapman quit the group when they started hang-gliding from the rims of active volcanoes. Everyone has their limits.

Journeys – long or short, on foot or by grand piano – are a part of our daily lives. While many are prosaic, such as a trip to the corner shop, when approached with a sense of novelty, imagination or Dadaist absurdism they can (quite literally in Chapman's case) catapult us in new directions. As you'll discover in *The Odysseum*, for some, even the daily commute can be an epic and surreal experience.

What constitutes an unconventional journey differs wildly throughout history and across cultures. For those living in the Middle Ages, the idea of walking into the wilderness for pleasure was anathema – such places were considered godless. The word 'heathen' was used pejoratively for anyone choosing to shun town or village life. Until recently, many of us viewed our urban hinterlands with similar disdain. Over the past 20 years, however, a growing interest in 'psychogeography' has led many to drift through industrial backwaters, edgelands and sewers in search of new meaning and connection. Writer and philosopher Alain de Botton is even fond of taking fellow seekers for a ramble around Heathrow Airport.

While we salute the intrepid travels of Charles Darwin, Ernest Shackleton, Captain Scott and the like, their stories are not to be found in *The Odysseum*. Instead, we seek out more bizarre and unfamiliar tales, as well as delving into the psychological impact of such journeys. These really are the paths less travelled.

We begin with Nazi architect Albert Speer who spent 11 years walking around the world. During his 19,250-mile (31,000-km) ramble, Speer endured sweltering desert heat and the extreme cold of the Siberian tundra. He jostled with a surging crowd in Beijing and witnessed the Northern Lights transform the world around him into a 'phantasmagoria of snow and light'. He even became the first person to cross the Bering Strait in the dead of winter. Most remarkable of all, as you'll discover, Speer did all of this without leaving the confines of Spandau Prison in Berlin.

While Speer journeyed inwardly to preserve his mental wellbeing – fortifying his visualizations by poring over travelogues in the prison's library – for others, mental peregrinations can result in an unravelling of the mind. In 1979 myriad journeys unfolded after artist Kit Williams instigated the world's biggest treasure hunt thorough his book *Masquerade*. While many of the 2 million people taking part remained armchair sleuths, thousands of the more zealous 'Masqueraders' set off on monumental wild-goose chases, resulting in air-sea rescues, arrests for trespassing and, for some, a slow descent into madness. The eventual uncovering of the treasure was so cloaked in subterfuge it remains worthy of the plot of a John le Carré novel.

Of course, we've also chosen to focus on extreme feats of physical endurance: the French doctor who deliberately drifted across the Atlantic Ocean to prove that he could survive at sea on saltwater, plankton and freshly squeezed fish; the men who packed themselves into crates and posted themselves around the world; and an unfortunate paraglider sucked up to 30,000 feet (9,144 m) by a storm cloud.

But perhaps some of the most unusual and fascinating journeys we unearthed revolve around totems: personal odysseys with objects that don't have to make sense to anyone other than the travellers themselves. When artist Grayson Perry embarked on a pilgrimage to Bavaria with his teddy bear, Alan Measles, he did so to make peace with the German people, after demonizing them in his childhood games. Motivated by a similar desire to lay past ills to rest, when his father passed away film-maker Andrew Kötting decided to take a giant, inflatable 'Deadad' on a tour around the world, inflating and then deflating his father at 65 places that held significance to them both.

Finally, it's been intriguing to unearth tales of famous body parts that have been on unlikely adventures after parting from their hosts. Rasputin's penis, in case you're interested (we know you are), went on an epic tour of Europe following the peasant-turned-holy man's assassination in 1916, spending time being worshiped as a holy relic in Paris before being swapped for a sea cucumber. As for the travels of Einstein's brain, Evita's mummified corpse and Hitler's jaw, well, you'll have to read on to find out ... *DB & JT*

Journeys of confinement

Albert Speer: the Nazi who walked around the world | Xavier De Maistre: the writer who voyaged around his bedroom

Solitude, deep snow, forest. I am several hundred km north of Okhotsk. Endless forests surround me; in the distance are smoking volcanoes with glaciers snaking down them... Approximately two thousand km more before I must make the crossing at Bering Strait, where I ought to arrive in about sixty weeks.
Diary extract, 17 April 1962

Albert Speer, 1905–1981

On 19 March 1955 – his 50th birthday – a lone traveller completes a 75-mile (120-km) walk from Berlin to his home town of Heidelberg in Germany. Thirty dried peas nestle in his trouser pocket, essential to the success of his journey. But the pilgrimage has provided little salvation for his tormented soul. In desperate need of further distraction, the traveller later mentions to an acquaintance that he plans to continue his walk, taking in Munich, Vienna, Rome and Sicily.

'Why stop there?' the acquaintance asks. The traveller admits that he would willingly walk all the way to Asia were it not for the communist countries of the Balkans blocking his way. He is no fan of these totalitarian regimes.

His acquaintance proffers an alternative route, via Greece and Yugoslavia (overlooking the fact that this, too, was communist). From here, he suggests, the traveller could then cross Turkey into Afghanistan, then India and Iraq, traversing great deserts to Iran and beyond. The suggestion is met with enthusiasm.

'I hope I find oases,' the traveller muses. 'At any rate, I have a good programme now. It should do me for the time being; it's a distance of more than 4,000 kilometres [2,485 mi]. You've helped me out of an embarrassing predicament.'

The journey would take nearly 11 years to complete, the traveller braving sweltering desert heat, enduring the extreme cold of the Siberian tundra, crossing the Bering

The gated entrance to Spandau Prison, Berlin, photographed in 1986. Constructed in 1876, the prison was demolished shortly after its last inmate, Rudolf Hess, died in 1987.

Strait in the middle of winter and becoming the first European to walk all the way to America by foot, before finishing his journey in Mexico. He will eventually walk over 19,250 miles (31,000 km). And yet in doing so Albert Speer – or Prisoner No. 5, as our traveller was better known – never actually left his garden.

LONG-TERM CONFINEMENT can drive us to do strange things. Or, to be more accurate, it can make us do things which might appear strange to those who've never been in such an unhappy predicament. Being deprived of basic comforts, external stimuli and intimate human contact can send some to the depths of madness and despair. Even the most stoical individual will devise strategies to 'kill time' – means of dealing with the frustrations and boredom brought on by long years of incarceration. Finding a hobby, writing a diary, learning a new language or embarking on an epic project are common means of salvation. Albert Speer – a high-ranking Nazi, architect and close friend of Hitler – had every need for such strategies.

Born into a wealthy and influential family, Speer was an ambitious young man. Following in his father's footsteps, he studied architecture at university. In 1931, during his studies, Speer decided to join the Nazi Party. With the help of an influential friend, Speer was given his first job by Joseph Goebbels to renovate the

Nazi Party's headquarters. From here it was a meteoric rise to success for Speer, and in 1934 he became the chief architect of the Third Reich. Speer would design and build many of Hitler's key monuments and lay out plans for Germania, a city to rival ancient Rome, to be built on the site of Berlin after the Germans had won the war. In line with Hitler's love of epic classical structures, Speer developed his 'Ruin Theory' designing and erecting colossal buildings that – like the ruins of Rome – he believed would keep their beauty even after their initial purpose had fallen to the wayside.

Speer was Hitler's blue-eyed boy. He stage-managed Nazi rallies, pioneered the use of searchlights at these spectacular gatherings and, by 1942, had been made Minister for Munitions. Speer made a point of paying a final visit to Hitler in his bunker, shortly before the Führer took his own life. He was one of the most powerful men in the Third Reich. That Speer was ignorant of the Final Solution – the industrial-scale murder of millions of Jews – as he always claimed, seems inconceivable now.

During the Nuremberg Trials, Speer was found guilty for his ruthless use of slave labour and concentration camp inmates as Minister for Munitions. In 1946 he joined Erich Raeder, Karl Dönitz and other high-ranking Nazi officials to serve long sentences in Berlin's Spandau Prison. Unlike the majority of his prison companions – known as the Spandau Seven – Speer repented for his role in the Nazi atrocities, though later in his prison diaries would also berate himself, writing: 'I wonder sometimes at my recklessness in assuming responsibility for the whole policy of the regime.' During his stretch, Speer would secretly pen a memoir of his time in the Third Reich, keep up a 20-year diary, design a Californian summer house for one of the guards and create an immense 'memory' garden. Only then was he ready to walk the world.

SPEER'S INCARCERATION began in October 1946. Right from the off he began his secret diary, which he kept up until his last day in Spandau. 'Days go by without interest in anything,' he wrote in the first week. 'If I go on in this twilight state I foresee that my resistance will totally disintegrate' (Albert Speer, *Spandau: The Secret Diaries*, 1975).

Over the first two years, Speer's clandestine scribblings on scraps of paper and toilet roll were smuggled out of Spandau. Decades later they would form the basis of what would become an international bestseller, *Inside the Third Reich*.

Recognizing the benefits to his sleep, energy levels and mental wellbeing, Speer also turned his attention to gardening. By 1948 he had transformed 1,125 square yards (6,000 m^2) of the prison yard into a garden full of nut trees and huge lilac bushes. He designed a promenade, laid flowers beds and a rock garden, planted fruit trees and tended a vegetable plot (though prison rules did not permit him or his fellow prisoners the right to consume the produce).

To stay healthy, Speer established a strict fitness regime, walking round and round his garden. He calculated that 30 circuits equated to 7 kilometres (4.3 miles) a day. Rudolf Hess, the only lifer in Spandau, offered Speer 30 dried peas to keep in his pocket, and suggested transferring them from one pocket to another as a means of keeping count.

Out of this small but significant act, Speer was struck by the idea of calculating how many circuits he would need to walk to his home of Heidelberg, and, with his peas in his pocket, set out to accomplish this over a number of weeks. At the end of the experiment, he noted that merely counting the kilometres was 'too abstract' but was struck by the idea of learning about and visualizing the places he could walk to.

Using a slide rule, Speer's friend at the prison library calculated the figures for the first set of distances he needed to cover: Vienna to Budapest to Belgrade: 615 kilometres (382 mi); Belgrade to Sofia to Istanbul: 988 kilometres (614 mi). Speer obtained maps, history books, travelogues and guides to familiarize himself with the places he was to visit, to help him evoke the landscape and its flora and fauna, geology and climate. He also researched the cities, their people, culture, architecture, churches, museums and art. If he could develop sufficient imagination in picturing his journey, thought Speer, he might even be able to feel something like enjoyment of the novelties in store. To Speer, these were efforts at survival.

By 6 August 1955, Speer was three months into his world tour. A few weeks earlier he had written despondently about fighting boredom on the stretch from Salzburg to Vienna; several times he had felt on the verge of giving up, but on reaching Bulgaria he seemed in a better mood and even tried to evoke the smells of his journey, as he watched a shimmering heat wave.

The roads were sandy, there was seldom even a single shade tree, and the flies were a plague. I plucked a stem of lemon balm from our herb garden and crushed the leaves between my fingers. The strong odour intensified and the illusion of foreign places, tramping the roads, intensified.
Speer, Spandau: The Secret Diaries

By Christmas Eve, Speer had crossed from Europe into Asia, though his limited access to research material let him down. He struggled to imagine the vista of Istanbul with its myriad mosques and minarets. His diary extracts continued to veer from self-pitying torment and despair to occasional moments of light-hearted exuberance. Outside Kabul he noted: 'As long as I continue my tramping I shall remain on an even keel.' A few days later he bemoaned the 'continuation of this senseless hike'.

True to the Germanic stereotype, Speer was meticulous with facts and figures. His record walk for one day, he notes, is 24.7 kilometres (15.3 mi); his best pace is 5.8 kilometres per hour (3.6 mph). By 1957 he had clocked up an impressive 3,326 kilometres (2,066 mi) and increased his daily average to 9.1 kilometres per hour (5.6 mph).

Over a third of the way into his world walk, Speer crossed the Chinese border and by 1959 had reached Peking (Beijing). He didn't stay long. A demonstration at the Imperial Palace and constantly surging crowd caused him to flee the city. He later confessed this to be a 'joke' (humour was never Speer's strong point) admitting that it was pride and vanity that made him flee; research in library books had unearthed the unwelcome discovery that the imperial metropolis of Beijing was comprised of the kind of classical architecture that Speer himself had planned for Germania. The Chinese had got there first. The following day in his diary, with surprising insight

DISTANCES WALKED BY SPEER FROM SPANDAU

Destination	Date arrived	Approx. distance walked km (mi)	Number of prison circuits
Vienna	19 June 1955	598 (372)	2,563
Peking	13 July 1959	14,717 (9,144)	63,073
Vladivostok	4 May 1960	16,367 (10,170)	70,144
Fairbanks	12 August 1963	21,696 (13,481)	92,983
Seattle	21 December 1964	24,634 (15,306)	105,574
Mexican border	7 October 1965	26,730 (16,609)	114,557

and self-deprecation, Speer acknowledged his own architectural clichés. Perhaps he had gone too far, he mused: a tradition of 'megalomaniacal buildings' extends from antiquity all the way to the French Revolution after all.

Whether from paucity of research material or disdain for the place, Speer recorded little of his time in China and was glad to leave. Ahead of him lay a further four years, trekking through the frozen wildernesses of Russia and Siberia up to the Bering Strait. Or, put another way, quite a few more laps of his prison garden.

Xavier de Maistre 1763–1852

While Speer dealt with his predicament on a macroscopic level, fleeing the confines of his prison through a global journey in his imagination, 150 years earlier Xavier de Maistre, a member of the French nobility, found a very different approach to killing time during his incarceration – one that was the polar opposite to Speer's.

In February 1790, at the beginning of the French Revolution, de Maistre relocated from Paris to Turin, describing his beloved home as having transformed into 'the city of the antichrist'. While still enjoying the luxuries and status of his nobility, he found himself under arrest for taking part in an illegal duel. As punishment, de Maistre was confined to his room for 42 days and, like Speer, decided to embark on a unique journey and to diarize his experiences.

Unlike Speer, de Maistre's journey was microcosmic, light-hearted and inward-looking: a six-week jaunt around his room, contemplating anew his artefacts, furnishing, books, paintings and even his clothes. Rather than crossing the Bering Strait or Europe, de Maistre crisscrossed his way from bed to sofa, chair to desk. It was a journey 'without any rule or method'.

They have forbidden me to roam around a city, a mere point in space but they have left me with the whole universe: immensity and eternity are mine to command.
Xavier de Maistre, A Journey around my Room *[1829], 2004*

SPANDAU PRISON,
BERLIN, GERMANY

NORTH
ATLANTIC
OCEAN

Heidelberg
Munich
Vienna
Belgrade
Sofia
Rome
Sicily
Constantinople
(Istanbul)
Turkey
Iraq
Kabul
India

EUROPE

ASIA

Peking (Beijing)

East
China
Sea

Arabian Sea

Bay of
Bengal

Phili

AFRICA

SOUTH
ATLANTIC
OCEAN

INDIAN OCEAN

AUSTRA

Great
Australian
Bright

In a little under 11 years, Speer braved
sweltering desert heat, endured the
extreme cold of the Siberian tundra and
crossed the Bering Strait, before ending
up in Mexico: an (imagined) journey of
over 19,250 miles (31,000 km).

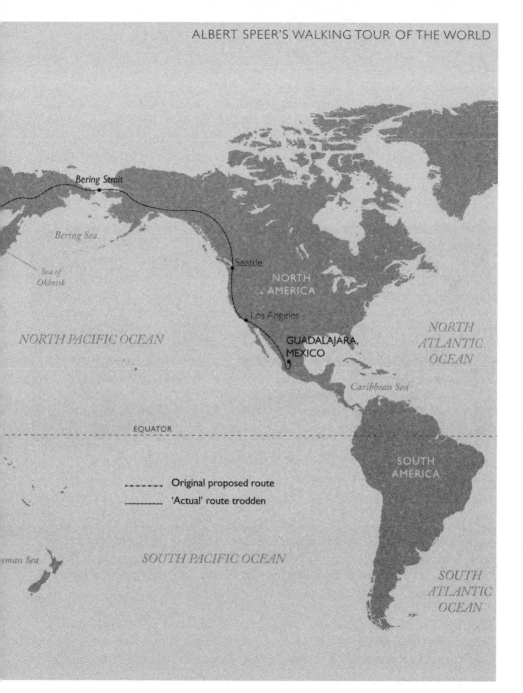

Bering Strait

Bering Sea

Sea of
Okhotsk

Seattle

NORTH
AMERICA

Los Angeles

GUADALAJARA,
MEXICO

NORTH PACIFIC OCEAN

NORTH
ATLANTIC
OCEAN

Caribbean Sea

EQUATOR

SOUTH
AMERICA

········· Original proposed route

————— 'Actual' route trodden

sman Sea

SOUTH PACIFIC OCEAN

SOUTH
ATLANTIC
OCEAN

Tongue firmly in cheek, de Maistre begins his journey by boasting that he has invented a new form of travel, one that is safe from robbers and open to the laziest of souls. Even the 'poor, sick and unadventurous' could manage such a journey, he excitedly proclaims.

Acknowledging a 'long journey to the desk ahead', de Maistre dons his travelling attire – pink-and-blue pyjamas – and begins by describing the basic dimensions and contents of his room before settling down to gaze affectionately at his sofa, joyfully reflecting on the many hours he has spent lolling on it. Observing the engravings and paintings on his wall he rhapsodizes over a Raphael portrait, before moving on to enthuse about the delights of music, and advise the reader that pink and white are the best colours for a bed.

Xavier de Maistre allegedly didn't think much of *A Journey around my Room*, but his elder brother Joseph – the philosopher and counter-revolutionary – arranged for it to be published, much to his brother's surprise (and to the delight of many modern readers).

Shuffling across the room in the chair he's still sitting in, he reaches his mirror to comment, 'It is here the lover practises his manoeuvres, studies his moves and prepares himself for the war he's about to declare; it's here he trains himself to make those lingering glances, those flirtatious expressions.' Shortly afterwards, de Maistre manages to fall out of his chair, noting how the fall has done the reader the service of shortening his journey by a good dozen or so chapters.

FAR FROM the discomfort and spartan surroundings that Speer would come to experience in Spandau, de Maistre has a servant to dress and feed him, and his faithful dog, Rosine, as companion. And while he had already served time in the army, his youthful exuberance seems untainted by the brutality of war, never once discussing the bloody revolution that has led him there. In fact, de Maistre comes across, at times, like a spring-loaded puppy, overpopulating his sentences with such a dearth of exclamation marks that you can't help but want to give him a shot of opium:

> Ah! What an aroma! Coffee! Cream! A pyramid of toast! Dear reader do have some breakfast with me!
> *de Maistre*, A Journey around my Room

Had they ever met through time and space, it's doubtful that de Maistre and Speer would have felt that they had much in common. Near the beginning of his journal, de Maistre writes of his dislike for people who have itineraries and ideas clearly mapped out. Indeed, his style couldn't be more antithetical to Speer's systematic cataloguing of events. Parodying the very idea of a grand tour – the fashion for young men to broaden their horizons with a jaunt around Europe – de Maistre determines to show 'only the cheerful aspects of his soul' and to journey by progressing, 'in short marches, laughing all along the way at the travellers who have seen Rome and Paris'. Such is his passion for metaphysics and allowing his thoughts to have free rein, he doesn't actually leave the confines of his armchair until the fifth chapter of his diary, when he finally stands up to contemplate his bed. He muses:

> Is there any theatre which arouses the imagination more, or awakens more tender ideas …? Isn't it a bed that a mother, overwhelmed with euphoria at the birth of her son, forgets the pains she has suffered? It is a cradle bedecked with flowers; it is the throne of love, it is a sepulchre.
> *de Maistre*, A Journey around my Room

Unashamedly horny, de Maistre does, however, on this rare occasion, rue his 'evil destiny' – acknowledging that he won't be getting his jollies on this 'throne of love' until his release.

A running theme during de Maistre's travels is the inner battles between heart and mind. His 'soul' and 'beast' come into conflict several times. On one occasion, he burns his hand on his fire tongs because his mind is elsewhere; on another, he berates himself for acting spoiled and impatient with his servant for no good reason.

Where Speer's journey is designed to distract himself from dark interior forces, de Maistre is unafraid to show his vulnerabilities, even if it is for comic effect. He ends the journey at his bookshelf and window in a contemplative mood, eulogizing on how his travels have made him see the world afresh and laments how few take the time to look upwards to admire the constellations. Here, at least, Speer would have concurred, writing nearly two centuries later: 'how I would like, just once, to go walking in the moonlight' (*Spandau: The Secret Diaries*).

WHILE THE GIDDY and playful nature of de Maistre's prose makes it easy to forget that he is under house arrest, it is the sheer power of Speer's imagination that enables the reader to forget, at times, that his world walk is a work of fiction. On occasion, like de Maistre, Speer addresses the reader directly, offering advice about how best to tackle the uninhabited wastes of Siberia, recommending that they catch the train at night. But don't sleep too much, he adds, as it would be a shame to miss the unending snowy mountain ranges and prairies. He advises that his reader open the top slat in their compartment window, to smell the freshness of the air. 'Only be careful,' he writes, 'if you expose your face too long, your mouth and nose will freeze.'

While Speer's walking average plummeted to 3 kilometres (1.8 mi) per day by 1962, he trudged on, still 60 weeks away from the Bering Strait. Two years later he was almost there, writing with awe, on New Year's Eve, of how the northern lights transformed the scenery into a 'phantasmagoria' of snow and light. So intense was his experience that he felt stunned to return to the gloomy facade of the prison.

The following year he walked the final few kilometres to the Bering Strait accompanied by Rudolf Hess, commenting to his bemused companion that they should be able to see the coast in a few minutes time. Speer had done his research, anticipating that the Bering Strait would be fully iced over, allowing him to walk across into Alaska and be the first European to reach America on foot. 'You know it really is a kind of mania,' Hess admonished Speer, half-jokingly. In a playful mood, Speer later discovered that he had actually been one kilometre out in his calculations – when he had been chatting with Hess, he was already on the ice of the Bering Sea. 'One has to be damn careful!' he writes.

By 1964 Speer reached Seattle; a year later, LA. Less than a year from release it must have seemed fitting that he was out of the frozen wasteland and closing in on civilization. A year later he was in Mexico – 'a dreary region' – and on the 18 September, 13 days before release, he finally submitted his all-important statistic: a world walk of 31,367 kilometres (19,490 mi).

Speer berated himself the next day for judging his fellow prisoners for having failed to set themselves such goals. What goal did he really have after all? Wasn't the sight of a man marching in a circle for decades more absurd than anything they could have done? A day later, he describes his walk as the greatest athletic achievement of his life.

Three days before release Speer weeded the garden for the last time, walked another 114 kilometres (70 mi) and he was gone, leaving the last remaining prisoner, Rudolf Hess, to live out the rest of his life alone in Spandau.

BEFORE INCARCERATION, the world Speer had known was one of war, fascism, fanaticism, brutality and, finally, defeat. By 1966 the new world he now entered was being reshaped by liberalism, pop music, sexual politics and drugs. 'Make Love Not War' was the motto of a new Western counterculture. While he could never have been prepared for such a culture shock, Speer did read voraciously in Spandau, even dabbling with the likes of Jean-Paul Sartre's Existentialist novel *The Age of Reason* (1945). Unsurprisingly, Speer could not make head or tail of it. The characters, more isolated in their loneliness than he had been in his cell, startled and perturbed him. Speer failed to see the irony that he was partly responsible for Sartre's philosophy. Both the communist regimes he abhorred and his own fascist party had forced its own people to participate in their misplaced utopian plans and enforced collectivism. Was it any wonder that a new philosophy should spring up rejecting everything but the rights and desires of the individual?

'Was it really the ambition to enter history that drove me on?' Speer wrote in Spandau in 1964. Certainly, his ambition never faltered. The publication of *Inside the Third Reich* six years after his release made Speer a media sensation and immensely wealthy. He didn't shy away from the publicity, appearing on TV and radio chat shows, openly discussing his sorrow and regret, while firmly denying any prior knowledge of the genocide. 'So many people expect me to offer justification for what I did,' he said in an interview in 1971. 'I cannot. There is no apology or excuse I can ever make. The blood is on my hands. I have not tried to wash it off – only to see it.'

Speer came to be dubbed by some as 'The Good Nazi'. In light of his close relationship with Hitler, and letters that have since proven his knowledge of the Holocaust and role in the persecution of the Jews, it's clear that Speer lied his way out of a death sentence. Tellingly, those hoping to get a real sense of the man through his diaries will be disappointed; all extracts were carefully edited and selected by Speer. There is relatively little reflection on himself, save occasional bouts of self-pity and claims that he was blind to the true machinations of the Nazi Party. While none of his buildings remain today, it's clear that Speer's real skill as an architect was the brilliance with which he constructed his public persona.

PERHAPS SPEER AND de Maistre are connected only through the novelty of their inner and outer journeys, seeking to escape their predicaments through two contrasting but novel walks. And yet there is a curious connection in the way both men chose to end their diaries – a reservation at being released.

De Maistre, giddy as ever, reflects on the pleasures he enjoyed as a result of his confinement:

Was it to punish me that they locked me up in my room – in that delightful country

that holds every good thing, and all the riches of life within its realms. You may as well exile a mouse in a granary.
de Maistre, A Journey around my Room

The day before his release, Speer wrote of his semi-erotic relationship to Spandau, and questioned whether he truly ever wanted to get away. After his release he, too, made a nocturnal journey to his old room – in his dreams. Speer had a recurring dream of returning to Spandau to visit someone he knew there and to attend to the neglected garden and untended paths. He walked his rounds, peas in pocket. After a few days he's ready to leave but is told he cannot; there has been a mistake. He remonstrates with the guards, reminding them of the 20 years he waited out in the prison, but the guards shrug. A general comes by for an inspection and Speer fails to mention that he is being held by mistake. When asked how he is being treated, Speer replies that he all is satisfactory. The general smiles at him.

In Spandau, Speer's imagination took him on an epic journey of escape. When freedom finally came, his imagination it seems, remained incarcerated in Spandau. *DB*

SEEKER'S DIRECTORY

Books
Spandau: The Secret Diaries, Albert Speer (Ishi Press, 1975)
Speer's extraordinary account of his 20-year incarceration at Spandau Prison, his role in the Third Reich and his relationship with Hitler.

A Journey around my Room, Xavier de Maistre (1794; Hesperus Classics, 2004)
De Maistre was placed under house arrest in Turin for 42 days after fighting an illegal duel. He wrote the manuscript during his confinement, then later penned a sequel, *A Night Voyage around my Room.*

Radio
Albert Speer's Walk around the World (2010), BBC Radio 4
Radio dramatization of Speer's imprisonment, during which he imagined a global journey to keep him sane.

X marks the spot

Kit Williams: the artist whose golden hare led to the world's biggest treasure hunt

Within the pages of this book there is a story told of love, adventures, fortunes lost, and a jewel of solid gold.
To solve the hidden riddle, you must use your eyes and find the hare in every picture that may point you to the prize.
Kit Williams, Masquerade, *1979*

During the summer of 1979 the artist Kit Williams and British TV presenter Bamber Gascoigne drove from London to Ampthill Park in Bedfordshire in the dead of night. Gascoigne, a fuzzy-haired boffin, was best known as host of the BBC programme *University Challenge*, a role he kept for over 25 years. Among the pair's possessions were a spade, a jewel-encrusted 18-carat golden hare sealed in a ceramic casket, and a fresh cowpat.

Once inside the vast country estate, Gascoigne and Williams headed to a cow-dung-spattered hill on which stood a large cross placed there in honour of Catherine of Aragon, Henry VIII's first wife. Desperately hoping that they wouldn't be disturbed or, worse, arrested, Williams dug a deep hole close to the cross and buried the casket. Gascoigne was present as a reliable witness to this furtive deed. After carefully replacing the soil and grass, Williams removed the cowpat from its container and asked his companion to place it on top – a cunning way of ensuring that in the weeks that followed, no passer-by would notice that the ground had been disturbed.

The burial of the casket marked the culmination of three years' intense artistic work for Williams. Along with casting the golden hare, he had created 15 intricate paintings for inclusion in a unique book, *Masquerade*, soon to be unleashed on the public. As well as telling a story with words and pictures, *Masquerade* was a complex treasure map, laced with cryptic clues that, once deciphered, would reveal the whereabouts of a golden hare valued at £5,000. If anyone had spotted Williams

Artist Christopher 'Kit' Williams now works as a figurative painter using traditional oil-painting techniques. He often hides mechanisms and moving parts within his works.

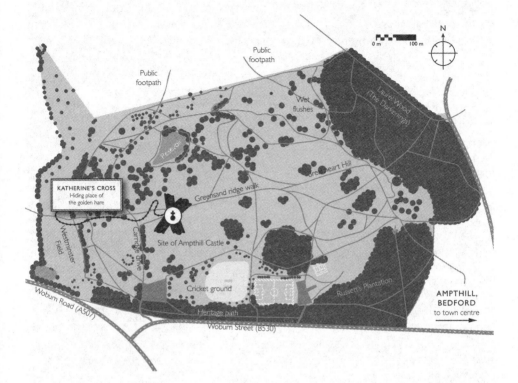

burying the hare that night, they could have undone the entire enterprise.

Williams's publishers, Jonathan Cape, initially printed 60,000 copies of *Masquerade*, optimistic that the book would capture the public's interest. They weren't wrong. By the time the golden hare was found 30 months later, over 2 million copies had been sold, catalysing the world's largest ever treasure hunt. Most of its readers remained armchair sleuths while the more zealous Masqueraders, as they became known, headed off on wild goose chases in their thousands, digging up half the country as they frantically sought for the treasure. There would be air-sea rescues, reports of trespassing, attempted bribes and accidents, and a handful of Masqueraders actually would be driven mad.

True to the piratical origins of an 'X marks the spot' map, the unearthing of the golden hare two-and-a-half years later was shrouded in skullduggery and deceit. But, despite the many thousands of players involved in this global hunt – and the travels they undertook – it would be the journey of the hare itself that proved to be the most surprising aspect of the hunt. And the most tragic.

IN THE MID-1970s Kit Williams was a rising star in the art world. It helped that Sir Elton John was an early collector of his work. When approached in 1976 by Tom Maschler – the chair of publishing house Jonathan Cape – to write a children's book, Williams had initially refused; he loathed the idea of creating a book that would be skipped through a couple of times and then forgotten. But the meeting with Maschler planted the seed of an idea. He was determined to create something unique: a treasure hunt in book form. In creating a sophisticated collection of visual puzzles, Williams reasoned that his readers would be forced to study the book closely and, in doing so, take the time to appreciate his art.

I would do something for my lost childhood. Real treasure, real gold, buried in cold, dark earth.
Kit Williams quoted in Bamber Gascoigne, *Quest for the Golden Hare, 1983*

Masquerade tells the story of a celestial love affair. The hero of the tale is Jack Hare, who is given the important task of delivering a jewelled necklace as a token of love from the moon to the sun. Jack travels through earth, air, fire and water on his journey but, being a bit of a klutz, somewhere along the way he loses his bounty. It was left to the reader to decipher the clues that Williams had hidden in the book and find out where the necklace had gone.

The three years Williams spent creating *Masquerade*'s artwork and golden hare also included serious time spent conceiving the story and the logistics of how the puzzles could work. He still wanted *Masquerade* to be accessible to children, as per the original brief, and wrote in the introduction that a bright child of ten could find the treasure, provided they had a basic grasp of mathematics and astrology. The only historical knowledge needed to solve the puzzle was in the line 'In the Earth am I one of six to eight', a reference to Catherine of Aragon. As for where to leave the golden hare, Williams couldn't risk burying it where it might be accidentally dug up or built on, so he chose a country park in a 'boring part of England'.

When you created the book, you created us.
Letter to Kit Williams quoted in Gascoigne, Quest for the Golden Hare

WITHIN SIX MONTHS of its publication in September 1979, *Masquerade* went from being a national obsession to a global one. It sold across Europe, Australia and even Japan. Half a million copies were bought in the USA alone, inspiring Laker Airways to set up ten-day *Masquerade* tours to the UK. Included in the package was hotel accommodation, car hire, a shovel and a map of England. The Italians loved *Masquerade* so much that an Italian version was created, for which a copy of

Williams's golden hare was hidden beneath the heels of a giant statue of Neptune carved into a cliff in Monterosso al Mare in Liguria.

The sale of *Masquerade* outside the UK, however, posed a logistical problem for those who wanted to solve the puzzle and undertake the hunt, so Williams offered to cover the plane fare of anyone who came up with the correct solution but lived abroad. Some took this as an opportunity to simply post random guesses in the hope of stumbling on the right answer; a couple from Houston sent over 500 guesses. For the next two years, Williams received 250-odd letters every day. One unnamed Masquerader wrote to him daily, sending notes with random red and blue letters scattered across them. After a while, bits of the sender's breakfast began to appear in the envelopes too.

Some readers refused to take the concept of *Masquerade* literally, writing to Williams that the golden hare was 'in our hearts' or 'in the fireplace in the Garden of Eden'. Another believed that it was hidden in the interstellar records of the Voyager 1 space probe.

Over the years that followed, thousands of holes were dug on public and private land across England. Acts of trespassing were common. One woman spent a night in jail for scaling a fire-station fence. An enthusiastic Swiss gentleman travelled all the way to Cornwall in his search for the hare, only to get stuck halfway up a cliff and have to be rescued. The most commonly visited places included the Greenwich Observatory, Stonehenge and Haresfield Beacon in Gloucestershire. The latter became such a popular target for spades that Williams paid for a National Trust sign to be erected there, informing the public that the treasure was to be found elsewhere.

Some Masqueraders gained notoriety for their obsessional approach to finding the golden hare. One German man sold his home in order to move to the UK to search for the treasure full time. A London antique dealer, Fred Hancock, drove over 50,000 miles (80,000 km) and wore out his brand-new Audi in the process. Hancock visited Plymouth 12 times alone, certain that the golden hare was buried under a statue of Sir Walter Raleigh. Following another hunch, he dug up the epicentre of every single island in the Thames, to no avail.

TRAGICALLY, FOR a few, *Masquerade* sent them on a journey into madness.

> My son bought me a copy of *Masquerade* the last time he visited us. The next time he comes I think I will shoot him.
> *Letter from a Devonshire farmer quoted in Gascoigne,* Quest for the Golden Hare

While Williams's treasure hunt provided countless hours of delight, frustration and furtive digging for thousands of Masqueraders, it led a small number to suffer

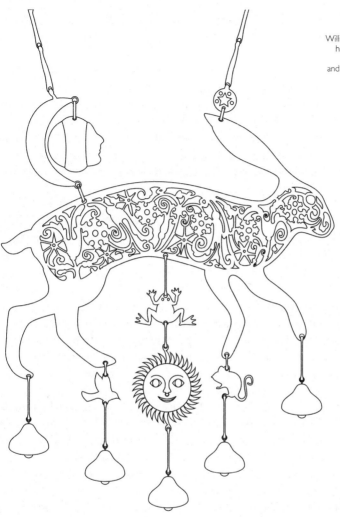

mental breakdowns. *Masquerade* was so tightly woven with images and words that patterns and connections – meaningful or otherwise – could be discovered everywhere. It didn't help that Williams deliberately planted red herrings; one conundrum led to the unveiling of the words 'Wrong, now try again.'

Two years after the hare was finally found, Richard Dale wrote of his experiences in a 117-page letter to Bamber Gascoigne, entitled 'Confessions of a *Masquerade* Loony'. Following a false trail, Dale believed that the treasure was located in drainage works in Hounslow. He travelled there and found and removed a ceramic plug roughly the same size as the golden hare's ceramic casket and became convinced that he'd found Williams's treasure.

Proof of the pudding were the initials 'KW' faintly embossed on the plug. Dale believed that he had uncovered the 'real' masquerade – that Williams had deceived the world into thinking the jewel was a hare. Excitedly, he contacted the press and media. Their interest soon wore off after Dale revealed his ceramic plug and discovered that he was the only person who could see Williams's initials on it. It didn't matter: by now he was beginning to find secret messages, clues and coincidences that pointed to an omnipresent game in which he had the lead role. Like Carey's salesman in *The Truman Show*, Dale came to believe that everyone was in on it.

> I convinced myself that Kit Williams's book was a masquerade – performed in print, on television, involving perhaps hundreds of people in every country where the book had been published. The biggest masquerade in the history of mankind.
> *Gascoigne*, Quest for the Golden Hare

Convinced that he had to alert Williams to his discovery, Dale reasoned that he should send him something pretty special. He settled on a long strip of toilet paper on which he had transcribed the entire Sermon on the Mount from the Bible. Williams's persistent silence and the eventual unearthing of the golden hare did nothing to shake Dale's conviction. This was just another part of the game. He remained 'the keeper of the jewel of *Masquerade*'.

While Dale admitted near the end of his 117-page confession that he had sought psychiatric help, his final comments demonstrated that he was still far from well. One thing that had seemed incredulous, even to Dale, was that Williams alone could have masterminded such a lavish worldwide game. Instead, it had to be none other than crime author Agatha Christie. While her death in 1976 (three years before the release of *Masquerade*) should have been enough to persuade him otherwise, Dale believed that Christie's brilliant mind had devised the whole masquerade prior to her death and left the plans for its execution as part of her estate.

Another 'victim' was Ron Fletcher, who came to see meaning and patterns relating to *Masquerade* in everything around him, and believed that Williams was contacting him directly and sending him clues. How did he know this? Whenever Fletcher typed a letter to Williams he would appear to get confirmation in the form of clues or secret messages, via the media and other means, minutes or hours later. How could this be, if Williams hadn't yet received Fletcher's letter? The only possible solution was that Williams had found a way to pick up the vibrations from Fletcher's typewriter. Like Dale, Fletcher couldn't conceive that Williams was capable of orchestrating such a thing on his own; it had to come from a bigger power structure. His conclusion? 'If you really want to know, it has to involve the queen. It has to go as high as that' (quoted in *Quest for the Golden Hare*).

RATHER THAN secret messages, the key clue to unravelling the puzzle of *Masquerade* actually lay in one the opening lines of the book: 'To solve the hidden riddle, you must use your eyes.'

Williams's pictures contained animals and people. Using a ruler to follow their gaze via the longest digits on the left hand or limb revealed a series of letters along the borders of each page. Rearranged they unveiled the sentence: 'Catherine's Long Finger Over Shadows Earth Buried Yellow Amulet Midday Points The Hour In Light Of Equinox Look You'. Within this sentence is an acrostic (a word or phrase composed from the first letter of each word) that read: 'close by ampthill', with a few rogue letters thrown in for good measure.

The clue should have eventually led Masqueraders to the statue of Catherine of Aragon in Ampthill Park. The exact spot could then be found by following the shadow thrown by the monument at noon on either the spring or autumn equinox.

It may sound easy when you know the answer, but even brainbox Bamber Gascoigne couldn't decipher *Masquerade*, despite knowing where the hare was buried, and expressed his concern to Williams that it was highly unlikely to be solved by a nuclear physicist, never mind a 'bright boy of ten'. He had a point.

After two and a half years – and tens of thousands of letters later – on 19 February 1982, Williams got the missive he'd been waiting for: a diagram of the cross in Ampthill Park, and a short note ending with the line, 'I believe the hare to be in this area.' It was signed 'Ken' and included a phone number. Excitedly, Williams called the number. To his surprise, the voice on the other line sounded listless, bored almost. After telling Ken that he was correct about the location, Williams begins to quiz him about how he came to the solution. To his growing dismay, he realized that Ken understood almost nothing of the clues leading to the hare's location but had stumbled on it, seemingly, by luck. By this point, however, it was too late – the cat was out of the bag. Ken mentioned to Williams that he'd noticed other depressions around the cross, close to where he'd been digging, and expressed concern that others were close to finding the treasure. Williams advised him to go back and dig.

Over the next few days Ken returned to the cross at night, to no avail. However, he did notice that another big hole had been recently dug. Five days after his call to Williams, Ken finally turned up at Ampthill Park during daylight hours with a group of friends. Posing as workmen, they cordoned off the area around the cross and dug for several hours. The casket was finally unearthed from the pile of discarded soil made by the hole that Ken had spotted a few nights previously. The hunt was finally over:

the treasure had been unearthed.

The media – chomping at the bit to meet the new keeper of the golden hare – found Ken an elusive and unwilling participant. He refused to be interviewed except in full disguise, dressed in a dirty overcoat, dark glasses, hat, false moustache and pipe, arousing suspicion among the press and public alike. These suspicions proved to be well founded. The name he gave – Ken Thomas – was an alias for businessman Dugald Thompson. Not long after, *The Sunday Times* ran a story in which it claimed to have unearthed the real truth about how the hare had been found. Thompson had a business partner, John Guard, whose girlfriend Veronica Robertson just happened to be an ex-girlfriend of Williams. While the artist had kept the solution of *Masquerade* a closely guarded secret, his then-partner had accompanied him on an early visit to Ampthill Park and, putting two and two together, had encouraged Thompson and Guard to dig there. The newspaper revealed that Williams felt 'conned'.

THERE IS, HOWEVER, a further sting in the tail. Remember the mysterious big hole that 'Ken' had noticed on his return to the cross? It had been dug by Mike Barker and John Rousseau, two research physicists at Sheffield University who, after 30 months of poring over *Masquerade*, had correctly solved the riddle, down to every last detail. Having visited Ampthill Park late at night on 18 February (the day before Williams received Ken's letter) the pair had dug in the correct spot but failed to notice the casket, perhaps owing to the darkness. Their correct solution reached Williams just a few days after Ken's letter. They claimed to be the rightful keepers of the jewel of *Masquerade* but were left empty-handed.

> It was the lowest point of my life.
> *Mike Barker quoted in Gascoigne,* Quest for the Golden Hare

As if things couldn't have got any more skullduggerous, in 1984 Thompson set up a software company, Haresoft, and used the golden hare as the prize for a new computer game, *Hareraiser*. It was an utter flop, with one player calling it 'quite possibly the worst game ever' and describing it as little more than a hare hopping across a field accompanied by a few oblique sentences. No one won the prize and the company eventually went into liquidation. In 1988 Thompson was forced to sell the hare and put it up for auction at Sotheby's. Williams, determined to get his treasure back, bid £6,000, but the hare sold for over £31,000 to an unnamed buyer and was flown off the Middle East never to be seen again. Well, almost.

IN ITS WAKE, the global success of *Masquerade* caused an inevitable avalanche of copycat books. In 1983 Cadbury's launched a 'Creme Egg Mystery' in a book called

Katherine's Cross, Ampthill Park. The precise location of the treasure was the spot at the edge of the shadow of the monument, at noon on the date of either the vernal or autumnal equinox.

Conundrum. The title, theme and artwork bore more than a passing resemblance to Williams's work: 12 paintings, with accompanying verses, contained clues to the whereabouts of 12 buried caskets, each containing an egg with a value of £10,000.

Like *Masquerade*, it proved to be immensely popular and not without controversy. Cadbury's was eventually forced to call off the hunt after being inundated with complaints from private land owners, and reports that certain sites of historical significance were taking on the appearance of a ploughed field. Another book, *The Piper of Dreams*, saw the burial – witnessed by the late, great Rod Hull and Emu – of a flute made of gold, silver and diamonds, but was something of a disappointment for its publishers when the treasure was unearthed within three weeks of its release and book sales dried up.

And what about Williams? At the height of *Masquerade's* popularity, the artist had toured America and appeared as a guest on popular British TV chat shows. However, being harangued by the public and press for three years, along with the scandal that followed the unearthing of the hare, began to take its toll. In the decades that followed, Williams became reclusive, choosing to sell his artwork only to friends.

WHAT WAS IT about *Masquerade* that ignited the public's interest and imagination? The treasure was valuable but it hardly compares to today's lottery prizes. Plus, many Masqueraders spent a small fortune in their searches; others risked their mental health. Perhaps the simple truth is that *Masquerade* served up the perfect ingredients of a ruddy good mystery.

It's worth noting that there has never been any documented evidence of piratical maps or parchments alluding to buried treasure; maps of 'X marks the spot' remain entirely in the realm of fiction. As children, however, many of us read books like *Five on Treasure Island* and yearned to have the kind of adventures experienced by Enid Blyton's young heroes and heroines and Timmy the dog. And in watching films like *Indiana Jones* or *Pirates of the Caribbean*, how many of us still feel that yearning?

In a *New York Times* interview in 1981, when asked about the process of creating *Masquerade*, Williams replied: 'It had to be romantic – a modern-day Holy Grail.' *Masquerade* was a call to adventure. It offered its readers a modern-day quest – a Holmesian mystery with a pot of gold at the end.

After the hare was unearthed, one its most zealous disciples, Fred Hancock, said: 'Personally, I like the idea of it all going on and on.' Hancock's disappointment wasn't so much that he hadn't won the prize but that the journey was over. It was a sentiment echoed by many.

The author and mythologist Joseph Campbell was fond of saying, 'It isn't the meaning of life we're all looking for but the experience of life' (*The Power of Myth*, 1988). For many, *Masquerade* had offered the experience of a lifetime, with one Masquerader writing to Williams, 'In all of my 72 years I can't recall having so much fun … what a jewel and lovely nut you are!'

The cryptic nature of William's treasure hunt also revealed something fascinating about the human psyche. Reflecting on the myriad solutions that Masqueraders had come up with (all of them wrong, bar one), Bamber Gascoigne wrote, 'Tens of thousands of letters from Masqueraders have convinced me that the human mind has an equal capacity for pattern-making and for self-deception' (*Quest for the Golden Hare*).

For Kit Williams, the golden hare was the necessary McGuffin to catalyse the story of *Masquerade*, yet this jewel of solid gold came to acquire its own journey of love, adventure and fortunes lost. After being buried underground for two and a half years, the hare spent six years in a bank vault only to be transported to Egypt where it has remained in obscurity for over 30 years. Its owner allegedly takes it out of security once a year to wear as a necklace on Christmas Day.

In 2009, however – the 30-year anniversary of the book's release – Williams was reunited with his golden hare when it was displayed at the British Film Institute for a few days before being returned to its owner in the Middle East. For Williams, it was an emotional affair. As for the golden hare, its journey, we suspect, is far from over. *DB*

Books

Masquerade, Kit Williams (Jonathan Cape, 1979)
A picture book, written and illustrated by Williams, that turned Britain into a giant treasure map.

Quest for the Golden Hare, Bamber Gascoigne (Jonathan Cape, 1983)
Gascoigne's account of the frenzied nationwide hunt for the jewel-encrusted golden hare.

Television

'The Man behind the Masquerade', BBC Four, 2009
A rare interview with Kit Williams, lifting the lid on life before and after *Masquerade*.

Atmospheric journeys

Larry Walters: the truck driver who flew away on his lawn chair | Lieutenant Colonel William Rankin: the pilot who fell through a storm cloud | Ewa Wisnierska: the paraglider sucked up to 30,000 feet | Auguste Piccard: the physicist who journeyed into the upper atmosphere

---

There is an art to flying ... learning how to throw yourself at the ground and miss. Clearly, it is this second part, the missing, that presents the difficulties.
Douglas Adams, The Hitchhiker's Guide to the Galaxy *(1979)*

Larry 'Lawnchair' Walters 1949–1993

What do you do if your life's ambition – to become a pilot with the US Air Force – gets shot down by poor eyesight? If you're Larry Walters, you take matters into your own hands. In 1982 the California truck driver, unperturbed by the stringent recruitment standards of the USAF, decided to take to the air in his own unique way: by attaching a large cluster of weather balloons to a lawn chair.

First, Larry and his girlfriend forged a requisition slip from his employer, Filmfair Studios, enabling them to purchase the 45 8-foot (2.4-m) weather balloons by saying they were to be used in a commercial. They then set about inflating the balloons and attaching them to Larry's patio chair. He put on a parachute, strapped himself in and took off, carrying with him only the absolute essentials – a pellet gun (to shoot balloons if he went too high), a CB radio, a camera, sandwiches and, most essential of all, a four-pack of beer.

The plan was to float 30 feet (9 m) above the Mojave Desert for a few hours, then effect a pleasant and gradual descent. To Larry's horror, however, the chair rose from his yard in San Pedro much faster than expected – he was eventually to reach a maximum altitude of 15,000 feet (4,600 m) – and was soon drifting over Los Angeles and into the primary approach corridor for Long Beach Airport, where he was spotted by several commercial airliners.

Unlike traditional hot-air balloons, where a single balloon is equipped with vents enabling altitude control, cluster balloons must be jettisoned, deflated or burst to allow for descent.

By this point, Larry had achieved his primary aim – to fly – but now faced the problem of how not to fly. Floating in LA airspace was not, he knew, going to make him very popular. Initially, though, he was too scared to shoot any of the balloons in case he unbalanced and fell from his madcap contraption. He tried getting in touch with REACT – a citizen's band radio monitoring organization. As he put it to them:

> … the difficulty is, ah, this was an unauthorized balloon launch and, uh, I'm sure my ground crew has alerted the proper authority. But, uh, just call them and tell them I'm okay.

After 45 minutes of literally hanging around, he eventually plucked up the courage to shoot a few balloons – just before the gun went overboard. Fortunately, the cull, as far as it went, proved sufficient to get him moving in the right direction. The slow descent concluded among power cables, blacking out an entire Long Beach neighbourhood for 20 minutes.

Upon picking him up, the Long Beach Police Department made a decisive statement: 'We know he broke some part of the Federal Aviation Act, and as soon as we decide which part it is, some type of charge will be filed.' Walters was eventually charged with 'operating a civil aircraft within an airport traffic area without establishing and maintaining 2-way communications with the control tower'. He was fined $4,000 – but his pilot's licence couldn't be suspended, since he didn't have one.

Having achieved his dream, Larry spent a short period as a motivational speaker and appeared on both *The David Letterman Show* and *The Late Show*. Eventually, however, he went back to a simple life – working for the United States Forest Service and as a security guard. He died in 1993, but will always be remembered as 'Lawnchair Larry', inspiring a song, various copycat flights and the 2003 Australian film *Danny Deckchair*, starring Rhys Ifans.

Larry was by no means the only weather balloon pilot – there have been many cases of people putting thin bits of rubber between themselves and an unpleasant meeting with terra firma. One such case was the Brazilian priest Father Adelir Antônia de Carli, whose 2008 foray into the atmosphere left him both wet and headless.

Seemingly well prepared – he was an experienced skydiver, and he'd trained extensively in survival skills prior to his launch – there was one huge gap in his safety plan, quickly exposed when he caught a breeze and got blown out across the Atlantic. While floating over the ocean, he rang the authorities from his mobile phone to ask someone to explain how his GPS equipment worked. Not long after that he lost contact entirely. A few months later, some of his balloons, along with the lower half of his body, were found floating in the sea.

On a happier note, Tom Morgan – a member of the Bristol-based League of Adventurists, reached a height of 8,000 feet (2,438 m) in October 2017 by tying 100 helium balloons to a camping chair and flying over the Sahara. He returned to Earth safe, dry and with all parts of his body intact.

Lieutenant Colonel William Rankin 1920–2009

Some of our atmospheric adventurers started their journeys in more conventional ways, only to return to Earth in a manner quite unexpected. This was certainly true in the case of Lieutenant Colonel William Rankin, the only person thus far to have fallen through a thunder and lightning storm and survived.

In 1959, at the controls of an F8 jet fighter, Rankin was on a routine return flight from South Carolina when engine failure forced him to eject from his aircraft. This, it might be noted, is a risky enough procedure in itself, notwithstanding the complications that would follow in Rankin's case.

As he was fired through the canopy and into the dark of the night, the air tore the seat from under him and the sudden decompression of his body burst blood vessels in his nose, eyes, ears and mouth, streaming blood that whipped away in the air. His eyes bulged, his abdomen ballooned, and every muscle in his body started cramping. Between flashes of the deep-purple void of space and the blinding whiteness of the sun, he glimpsed his stomach, swollen as if he were pregnant.

A US Navy lieutenant ejects from the cockpit of his Vought RF-8A Crusader in 1963.

Who, in that moment, could believe they would survive? As he fell, Rankin reached the cloud tops. At this altitude, it was around -40 °C (-40 °F), but he was still conscious, wheeling helplessly, limbs splayed apart and his oxygen mask flapping at his face. This meant – he realized – that he hadn't taken a breath since ejecting. Without oxygen he would black out or risk serious brain damage. So strong were the G-forces, however, that he couldn't move his arms to apply the mask.

Eventually, the air became denser and, finally, he was able to pull the mask over his face. He was still falling, though, and had no idea how long he'd been in the air: was he just coming through the clouds, or was he seconds from slamming into the ground?

When he felt hail tapping against his body, Rankin relaxed a little. Knowing that hail forms at around 10,000 feet (3,000 m), he had a way to go before he reached the Earth. Suddenly, his body lurched; he looked up to discover that his parachute had opened early. Fortunately, it seemed to be working. With relief, Rankin used this

'Cloud suck' is a dangerous phenomenon that can happen when a paraglider experiences significant lift due to a thermal under the base of cumulus and cumulonimbus clouds.

opportunity to check his body and equipment for damage. Apart from a deep cut on his finger, everything seemed to be in order.

As he hung below his parachute, he noticed that there was less pressure and more turbulence again. Why? A clash of thunder reverberated through his body. Lightning seared against his eyelids. The cloud roared. His question was answered: he was in the middle of the storm – blades of blue seemed to scissor through him. What if one struck the canopy? He looked up and saw it illuminated like a vast domed cathedral.

Worse still, the cloud was so full of rain that he was drowning. He held his breath, imagining the prospect of his body found hanging from some tree with his lungs full of water. How would they explain that?

He looked at his watch. It was 18:20. How had 20 minutes passed? He realized that he was trapped in the storm cloud, as helpless as a hailstone, buffeted back up into the top of the cloud to run the gauntlet once again. How long for? He remembered the weeks-long storms he'd witnessed at the naval station in Guantanamo Bay. Of all things, would he die of starvation?

He was jerked violently up into his chute. The clammy silk engulfed him like a wet bedsheet, but somehow it released him again. The risers went taut once more, and he could see that the parachute remained open and whole. If it could survive, he reasoned, so could he.

He'd been in the cloud for 40 minutes when at last it let him go; if not a moment too soon, though, it was a little too quick – the storm spat him out over an area of wooded land, too fast for a safe landing. As trees came up to meet him, he braced for impact – but the boughs proved his salvation, slowing his final descent and allowing him to hit the ground conscious and thankful to be alive.

Rankin was treated for frostbite, bruises and severe decompression. No one else was hurt; the empty F8 had come down harmlessly in a field. The pilot went on to write a first-hand account of his experiences in the book *The Man Who Rode the Thunder* (1960).

Ewa Wiśnierska 1971–

Rankin hasn't been the only person to get buffeted around in bad weather. In 2007 Ewa Wiśnierska was in Australia, training for the Paragliding World Championships near Manilla, New South Wales, when a storm sucked her in and up to an altitude of nearly 30,000 feet (9,144 m) – higher than Mount Everest.

Paragliding involves gliding through the air attached to a wide canopy. Unlike hand-gliding, there is no hard structure; it looks somewhat like a sleeping bag attached to a large sling – a fairly flimsy kit for storm-exploring.

Ewa flew upwards at a rate of 66 feet (20 m) per second, as helpless as a leaf, watching lightning flash all around her. At some point in the journey she passed out, an eventuality which, according to doctors, probably saved her life. At that height, oxygen levels would be dangerously low, and the temperature could be in the region of -40 °C (-40 °F); her body would have had little or no time to adjust. In addition, hailstones would have been forming around her – ranging in size from apples and oranges to small melons.

The fact that she and the canopy of her glider remained intact at all was nothing short of a miracle. A Chinese competitor, by the name of He Zhongpin, flew into the same storm, but he was not so lucky. Rescue helicopters found his body 47 miles (75 km) away from his initial launch site.

Data from her instruments suggests that Ewa was thrown around by the storm for about an hour, though, of course, she herself was not conscious for much of this time. She was whisked up at a speed of 67 feet (20 m) per second (from about 500 ft to 33,000 ft – 760–10,000 m – in 15 minutes) and finally landed 3.5 hours later.

At 20,000 feet (6,100 m) Ewa awoke and was able to fly her glider back down to safety; she was found to be covered in ice, with multiple bruises all over her body – on top of which she nearly lost her ears to frostbite. The president of the Manilla Sky Sailors Club said that her survival was like 'winning the lottery ten times in a row'.

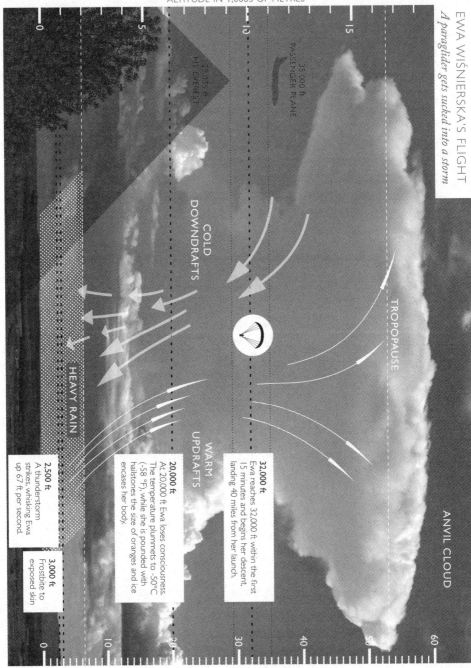

EWA WIŚNIERSKA'S FLIGHT
A paraglider gets sucked into a storm

29,035 ft
(MT EVEREST)

35,000 ft
PASSENGER PLANE

COLD
DOWNDRAFTS

TROPOPAUSE

HEAVY RAIN

WARM
UPDRAFTS

ANVIL CLOUD

32,000 ft
Ewa reaches 32,000 ft within the first
15 minutes and begins her descent,
landing 40 miles from her launch.

20,000 ft
At 20,000 ft Ewa loses consciousness.
The temperature plummets to -50°C
(-58 °F), while she is pounded with
hailstones the size of oranges and ice
encases her body.

2,500 ft
A thunderstorm
strikes, whisking Ewa
up 67 ft per second.

3,000 ft
Frostbite to
exposed skin

ALTITUDE IN 1,000S OF FEET

42

HOW FAR WE'VE COME (AND GONE)
The up and downward journeys of sky explorers

Name	Date	Method	Altitude	Outcome
Felix Baumgartner	14 October 2012	Skydive from helium balloon in the stratosphere	38,969.3 m	Safe landing, broke record.
Auguste Piccard & Paul Kipfer	27 May 1931	Aluminium gondola, attached to a helium balloon	15,781 m	Emergency landing on a glacier with one hour's supply of oxygen to spare.
He Zhongping	14 February 2007	Paraglider sucked into a storm cloud	5,900 m	Struck by lightning and died.
Larry Walters	2 July 1982	One lawn chair, 42 weather balloons	4,600 m	Safe but precarious landing, $1500 fine and a dream come true.
A sheep, a duck & a cockerel	19 September 1783	A cotton canvas hot air balloon	600 m	Safe landing, landmark moment in history as the first hot-air balloon flight.
Clément Ader	11 August 1890	The Ader Éole (also called Avion), a steam-powered Bat-Plane	8 inches	First time a powered aircraft carrying a human being made a take-off from level ground. Safe landing.

Auguste Piccard 1884–1962

A final, brighter story is that of Auguste Piccard, who not only reached the heady heights of 75,459 feet (23,000 m) but was instrumental in enabling his son, Jacques Piccard, to explore the Mariana Trench located in the western North Pacific at a depth of 35,813 feet (10,916 m).

If one sought to picture a stereotypical scientist and inventor, Swiss-born Auguste Piccard would more than likely be the result. In fact, he was a major inspiration for Hergé's Professor Calculus in *The Adventures of Tintin* – except that, unlike Calculus, Piccard was particularly tall with an 'interminable' neck; Hergé recorded that he reduced the fictional scientist's size in order to fit him into the panels with the other characters.

Piccard designed a spherical, pressurized aluminium gondola that could be attached beneath a helium-filled balloon. The reason? To explore the upper reaches of our atmosphere in order to measure cosmic radiation, with which he had become obsessed. The gondola allowed him to withstand the high pressures exerted on the human body without the need to wear a specialized suit.

Though the initial flight was successful, the journey was not entirely uneventful: the ball began to leak during the ascent and, in panic, the two occupants used Vaseline and cotton waste to plug it. In addition, after observing the world from 10 miles (16 km) high as a flat disc with upturned edges, the voyagers found that they could not descend. They were left hanging on the edges of space while they waited for the cool evening

Auguste Piccard's 'nacelle', which would carry him into the stratosphere. The spherical aluminium capsule was pressurized to allow ascent to high altitude without a pressure suit, but just in case he needed more protection Piccard also had a helmet made from sewing baskets and pillows.

In the 1930s, William Beebe and Auguste Piccard began developing a deep-sea diving 'ball' capable of withstanding enormous pressure and allowing humans to descend thousands of feet into the depths of the ocean.

air to make the gas in their balloon contract. All the while, their oxygen tanks were emptying, and by the time they landed near the Grosser Gurgler Ferner glacier in Austria, they were down to their last hour of breathable air.

The science behind the gondola then inspired a bathyscaphe (a free-diving self-propelled deep-sea submersible, suspended below a float) which, in 1960, took Auguste's son Jacques, along with Lieutenant Don Walsh, down to a depth of 35,800 feet (10,911 m). While, thankfully, Piccard junior's craft didn't leak, there was a loud crack heard by the crew when they reached a depth of 30,000 feet (9,144 m). Not to be put off by unidentified ominous noises, they continued the descent and landed on the bottom of the Mariana Trench. They stayed there for 20 minutes before deciding that cracks in the viewing windows might be a good reason to start heading back up. A rebuilt version of the underwater craft later located the remains of two lost US Navy nuclear submarines.

And what of the future? Well, there's still plenty of space in the weird-and-remarkable-flights hall of fame. Perhaps the next candidate will be Bart Jansen, who's put on record his desire to make a helicopter from a dead cow. Speaking in 2016, he said: 'If I'm going to fly, I want to fly in something weird. We've been thinking about animals that are big enough to fly in.'

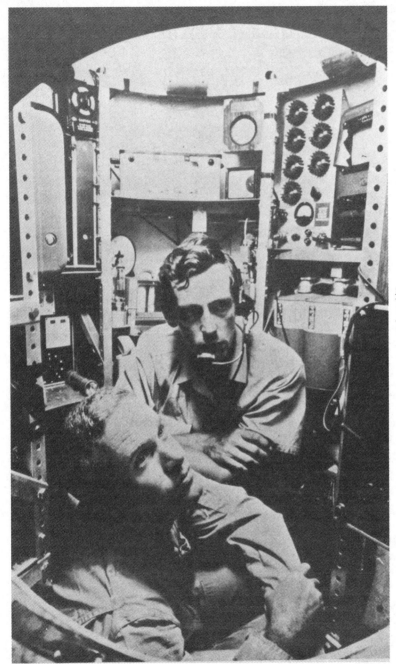

Jacques Piccard in
the bathyscaphe
Trieste, while
descending into the
Marianas Trench, 1960.

This won't be Jansen's first foray into bestial aviation – he started with his beloved cat, Orville (named after one of the Wright brothers), and has since pressed drone technology into the service of creating flying sharks, flying ostriches (yes, really), and flying rats. A flying golden retriever and a badger submarine have also been prototyped. Yes, if Bart has his way, the Lawnchair Larrys will in time have to make room (or rather 'air space') for some Bovine Bartys. Oh, and local zoos have no need to be concerned – all animals used so far have died from natural causes, and Jansen has a waiting list of eager ex-pet owners looking forward to the immortalizing day when Fido, Polly and Whiskers are swept up, up and away. *JR & GL*

SEEKER'S DIRECTORY

Books
The Man Who Rode the Thunder, William Rankin (Prentice Hall, 1960)
Lieutenant Colonel William Rankin is the only known person to have survived a fall through a cumulonimbus thunderstorm cloud. This is the first-hand account of his experience.

The Adventures of Tintin, Hergé (1929–76)
Inventor and explorer Auguste Piccard, who explored the upper reaches of our atmosphere while attached to a helium-filled balloon, was a major inspiration for the character Professor Cuthbert Calculus in *The Adventures of Tintin* series.

Film
Danny Deckchair (dir. Jeff Balsmeyer, 2003)
Hapless construction worker Danny takes to the air in a deckchair rigged with helium-filled balloons and returns to earth a hero. Inspired by the true antics of 'Lawnchair Larry' Walters.

Up (dir. Pete Docter, 2009)
Elderly widower Carl Fredricksen fulfils his dream to see the wilds of South America by tying thousands of balloons to his house.

Totemic journeys

Andy Warhol: the artist who sent his penis to the moon | Grayson Perry: the ceramicist who motorcycled across Bavaria with his teddy | Werner Herzog: the film-maker who dragged a 320-ton steamboat over a hill

When embarking on a journey of any length, we are never entirely alone. There are always those all-important possessions that join us for the ride – washbag, clothes, shoes, mobile – and the things we curse ourselves for forgetting. More curious perhaps are the totemic items that we also choose to take with us on our travels such as keepsakes, charms, memorabilia: personal objects that may have no practical purpose but, for us at least, are charged with meaning.

People of faith may carry a crucifix, rosary beads, a copy of the Koran or a figurine of Ganesh. For soldiers heading to war, pictures of their sweethearts are often essential totems; in the days before photography, they might have taken a lock of their loved ones's hair. Notoriously superstitious, many sailors still carry charms and amulets to ensure a smooth voyage. Once, a highly prized talisman for mariners was a birth caul – the membrane that sometimes covers a newborn baby's head – taken on sea trips as protection against drowning.

One illustration of our attachment and need for totems can be seen in the objects that US astronauts chose to take with them on their trips to the moon. During the three years of Apollo missions, astronauts were severely restricted as to what personal items they could take on their voyage, and so were provided with a small 'personal allowance pouch'.

While it's widely known that Neil Armstrong left a gold olive branch on the moon as a symbol of peace during the historic moon-landing of 1969, NASA – fearing an atheist backlash – chose not to make it public knowledge that Buzz Aldrin had packed a miniature chalice, some wine and bread. Shortly before Armstrong stepped out onto the lunar landscape, Aldrin took out his sacred items, requested a moment's silence and read from the Gospel of John: 'I am the vine, you are the branches. Whoever remains in me, and I in him, will bear much fruit; for you can do nothing

without me.' The first time that liquid was poured on the moon was a sacred rite, an act of communion.

'At the time I could think of no better way to acknowledge the enormity of the Apollo 11 experience than by giving thanks to God,' Aldrin was later reported to have said. While Armstrong claimed to observe a respectful silence, it's more likely he was silently rehearsing his immortal words for the giant leap that was about to follow. He still managed to fluff them up.

Moon astronauts

Many astronauts, like Charles Duke on the Apollo 16 mission, chose to take a family photograph on their flight to the moon. Duke was unique, however, in opting to leave his photograph behind on the moon's surface. It bore a picture of himself, his wife and their two kids sitting on a bench. On the back Duke wrote: 'This is the family of

Astronaut Duke from Planet Earth. Landed on the Moon, April 1972.' While the lack of atmosphere on the moon ensures that any objects left are preserved, sadly this wasn't quite the case with Duke's photograph. Whether he was aware of it or not, the intense sunlight and solar radiation on the moon soon bleached Duke and his family out of existence.

Famously, astronaut Alan Shepherd managed to persuade NASA to let him take a club and two golf balls with him on the Apollo 14 mission in 1971. While he fluffed the first shot, the second allegedly went for miles. It may well have been the longest drive in history; scientists have calculated that, if hit well, the ball could have stayed in the air for over 70 seconds and travelled roughly 2.5 miles (4 km).

The most surprising object to have made a pilgrimage to the moon, however, has to be Andy Warhol's penis. Unbeknown to the crew of the Apollo 12, one of the engineers for the lunar module had attached a piece of art to its leg. 'Moon Museum' was a tiny ceramic chip (three quarters of an inch by half an inch) containing six

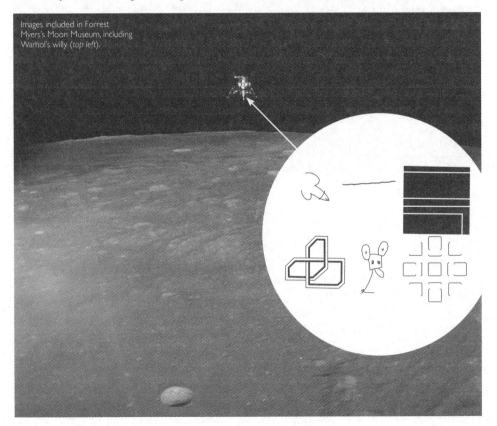

Images included in Forrest Myers's Moon Museum, including Warhol's willy (*top left*).

illustrations. It was created by Forrest Myers and included work by himself and five other New York artists including Warhol.

While the Pop artist liked to pretend the image was his stylized signature, it's unequivocally a neatly doodled willy. When Myers first heard of the moon landings he had an overwhelming urge to be the first artist to have a tiny museum on the moon, and approached an engineer friend who was working on the lunar module. Myers persuaded him to fasten the museum to one of the module's legs. As the vehicle was left on the moon, the museum remains there too. Richard Kupczyk, the launch pad foreman for the lunar module, later confessed that some of his crew also buried photos of their children and wives within the blankets that surrounded the lunar module.

A secret art gallery, a doodled knob, golf balls, family photographs and religious items probably say more about what makes us uniquely human than the carefully chosen sounds, music and images that accompany Voyager 1 and Voyager 2 on their respective journeys 10 billion miles (16 billion km) into the cosmos. The famous Voyager Golden Records include images of our solar system, DNA and an illustration of a naked couple that caused so much controversy at the time that it was eventually reduced to a simple outline.

Commenting on the objects secreted on the lunar module, TV presenter Gwen Wright, said: 'The hard-working team … who had built the moon lander, had shown a playful willingness to bend some rules, making the space project more profoundly human than I had ever realized' (Gwen Wright, *History Detectives*, Episode 801).

Grayson Perry 1960–

> Stunt double teddy bear wanted.
> *British Museum advert, 2011*

In 2011 The British Museum launched a competition to find a stunt double teddy bear. The winning toy was for a new exhibition, 'Tomb of the Unknown Craftsman', curated by Turner Prize-winner and ceramicist Grayson Perry, well known for making public appearances as his dazzling alter-ego Claire. At the heart of the exhibition Perry wanted to display his childhood teddy bear, Alan Measles, but the artist was so attached to the toy that he'd requested a doppelgänger to take its place.

Alan Measles had been given to Perry on his first Christmas in 1960. The toy took its full name from an infant friend of Perry's, combined with a bout of measles that he had contracted around the same time. In Perry's young imagination, Alan had taken on the role of a brave rebel leader, fighting against an imaginary German army. With the adult Perry happily married to a psychotherapist, it was perhaps inevitable that he would come to wonder whether a hated stepfather had provided the inspiration for the Nazi enemy in his young subconscious, with teddy bear Alan as his saviour. Perry certainly viewed Alan as a surrogate father.

> Onto him I projected all my positive male qualities. He was the benign dictator of my fantasy world and carrier of my own manhood throughout my childhood years. Now as an artist he's a god for me. A personal deity.
> 'Grayson on his Bike' (BBC Radio 4, 2010)

Over the decades, Alan became a grubby lump of yellow foam. He had also lost an ear during 'the great gas fire tragedy of '63' ('Grayson on his Bike'). He remained however, an important totem in Perry's life. To celebrate his 50th birthday, the artist decided that it was time to make peace with the Germans and 'lay the metaphor to rest'. Together, Alan and Grayson would embark on a road trip, a 'pilgrimage to the land of beer and sausages', to curtail his childhood demonization of the German people. For a professional artist and Turner-prize winner, the trip was inevitably conceived as an art project too.

As transport for the journey Perry had a 'non-macho' Harley Davidson motorbike custom-made at considerable expense. Nearly 10 feet (3 m) in length, and painted in powder blues and pinks, it bore the words 'humility' and 'patience' on either side. At the rear sat a glass-fronted shrine – a little Gothic chapel – inside of which sat Alan on a nickel-plated throne. Perry's outfit for the ride was equally flamboyant – a bright green helmet and a leather two-piece suit in lilac and yellow, with a red heart over his groin and a picture of Alan on his chest. Astride the bike Perry resembled a French cavalier crossed with a bag of Dolly Mixtures. It was an arresting sight.

Setting off from their home town Chelmsford, one man and his teddy bear began with a spin around Germany's famous Nürburgring racing track before winding their way across idyllic Alpine roads to Neuschwanstein, the iconic Disneyland-type castle once owned by Mad King Ludwig of Bavaria. As well as being 'a temple to kitsch' (Perry), the castle was also a location in the film *Chitty Chitty Bang Bang* (1968), which, Perry admitted, was part-inspiration for his equally kitsch motorbike.

From here, under Alan's insistence, the pair stopped off at the famous Steiff teddy bear factory in Giengen and finished at Backnang, Baden-Württemberg (twinned with Chelmsford), where Perry delivered a speech of goodwill on behalf of the people of his home town. While the whole escapade was largely a bit of self-indulgent fun, who couldn't have been dazzled by the arresting sight of Perry and Alan whizzing past them on the Harley like a cartoon villain and his sidekick from a lost Pee-Wee Herman film? For Perry the exhibitionist, the spectacle was the heart of the journey, 'to blur the line between fantasy and reality. Designing your own religious experience – the doing is the thing' ('Grayson on His Bike').

Grayson Perry's custom-built anti-macho motorbike, complete with a shrine to his beloved teddy bear, Alan Measles.

When Perry's 'Tomb of the Unknown Craftsman' exhibition opened at the British Museum, the following year, the pink-and-blue Harley Davison stood by the entrance. The curated exhibition offered visitors the chance to contemplate 190 man-made objects, created by unnamed but skilled craftsmen and -women. Alan Measles's stunt double was placed under glass in the centre of the exhibition. Did it really matter that Alan wasn't the real McCoy? As Perry saw it, whether we're on a pilgrimage with a cherished possession or taking a trip to see one in an art exhibition, it's not the authenticity of the objects themselves but the meaning we bring to them and the stories they hold.

Tony Hawks 1960–

Sometimes the objects we choose to accompany us on our travels may gain meaning and significance only when the journey reaches its end. It's easy to feel a sentimental attachment to a hat or a tatty old backgammon set after they've accompanied us on a round-the-world trip and have become imbued with some of the memories of our adventures. But can the same be said for everyday kitchen appliances? In 1995, while travelling through Ireland, comedian Tony Hawks was amazed to spot a man attempting to hitch-hike with a fridge. It became a well-told anecdote for Hawks until, two years later, after a drunken night with a friend Kevin, Hawks agreed to a bet: 'I hereby bet Tony Hawks the sum of One Hundred Pounds that he cannot hitchhike round the circumference of Ireland, with a fridge, within one calendar month.'

Thanks to extensive media coverage, it wasn't long into the journey that Hawks became the talking point of Ireland. During his travels, the fridge was baptised 'Saiorse Molloy' (*saiorse* is Irish for freedom), blessed by a nun and taken for a ride on a surf board. Both Hawks and the fridge became celebrities across Ireland. Hawks, of course, won the bet and Kevin dutifully flew to meet him in Dublin to hand over the £100. Having also bought Hawks a ticket for his fridge to fly, first class, back to London, Kevin swiftly took the £100 back as payment.

In 2017 Hawks planned to revisit his journey but had to postpone at the last minute, owing to family illness. When (or if) he does return to Ireland, for Hawks to take a different fridge with him would be unthinkable. While Perry was happy to have a stunt-double teddy bear in his exhibition, it had to be the real Alan Measles that accompanied him on his pilgrimage. And while a fridge is just a fridge, for Hawks not to take the one that surfed the Atlantic and gave him a best-selling book would be little short of heresy.

In 2006 litter pickers discovered the remains of a church organ near the top of Ben Nevis. It had been carried there 35 years earlier by former Highland Games athlete, Kenny Campbell.

The humour in Hawks's travelling with such a ludicrous and cumbersome item was echoed in 2006 by the discovery of the remains of what looked like a grand piano underneath a large cairn at the top of Britain's highest mountain, Ben Nevis. A discarded biscuit wrapper by the instrument suggested that it had been brought to the top of the mountain in the mid-1980s. The culprits finally revealed themselves to be two removals men, who admitted to having carried the piano to the top of the 4,413-feet (1,345-m) mountain in an effort to get into *The Guinness Book of Records*.

Despite repeated communication with the organization, when the pair finally reached the summit, no one showed up to officially qualify their achievement. With their mammoth task unproven, the piano was quietly placed beneath a large pile of stones and forgotten about. Travelling with a fridge or piano, however, is mere child's play when compared with the monumental task German film-maker Werner Herzog set himself in the 1980s, deep in the Amazon. Our final story is a reminder that – unlike Hawks's fridge – some objects that we chose to build a journey around can turn from totem into self-made curse.

Werner Herzog 1942–

'If I believed in the devil I'd say the devil is right here. Even if I get that boat over the mountain and finish the film, anyone can congratulate me into finding it marvellous but nobody on this earth will convince me to be happy about that. Not until the end of my days.'
Werner Herzog in Burden of Dreams *(dir. Les Blank, 1984)*

In 1978 German movie director Werner Herzog began work on his latest film, *Fitzcarraldo*. It is the story of an Irish entrepreneur, Brian Sweeney Fitzgerald, who, in the late 1800s, has a vision of building an opera house deep in the Peruvian jungle. To fund his dream, he hopes to take control of the last unclaimed area of the Amazon rich in rubber. It is unclaimed for good reason, being inaccessible by boat owing to dangerous rapids en route.

As a large steamboat is essential for transporting goods to and from his new territory, Fitzgerald, or *Fitzcarraldo* as he is known in Peru, formulates a plan to get close to it via a different river then – at a point where the two rivers almost meet – carry his steamboat a mile overland between the two waterways, to avoid the rapids. Despite many setbacks, with the help of hundreds of natives, Fitzcarraldo finally succeeds in getting the boat over the hill and into the second river. The following night, the superstitious natives, fearing that they have defied and displeased nature, release the boat from its mooring, sending it, and Fitzcarraldo, downriver into the rapids. The mission is abandoned. Making the best of a bad situation, our protagonist spends the remainder of his money in paying a visiting opera company to come and perform on his steamboat, shortly before he has to sell up. For Fitzcarraldo, it's a happy ending of sorts.

Herzog's *Fitzcarraldo* was half-based on truth. The real-life Carlos Fermin Fitzcarrald was a brutal and despotic rubber baron with no interest in opera. He did, however, dismantle a 30-ton boat and drag it over a hill between two rivers.

For the key scenes where Fitzcarraldo's steamboat is pulled overland, Herzog's backers had always presumed that the maverick director would use a plastic model. They should have known better – Herzog's films and documentaries penetrate into the psychological, physical and geographical extremities of life. The director's fanatical nature has often led him willingly into dangerous and inhospitable environments, taking less willing members of his film crew with him. In making *Fitzcarraldo*, Herzog wanted to capture the desperation, isolation and sheer willpower of his protagonist. He was never going to use a model or special effects for the big scene. Instead he proposed dragging an intact 320-ton steamboat over an impossibly steep hill and through a mile of impenetrable jungle. For Herzog, it would be a journey into the heart of darkness. Unlike Joseph Conrad's Marlow – journeying downriver in the Congo – 'the horror, the horror!' – what ultimately broke Herzog was not man's brutality but nature's.

FITZCARRALDO WAS CURSED from the start. Shooting began in 1979 close to the Peruvian and Ecuadorian border, with Jason Robards and Mick Jagger taking the lead male roles. When a border battle erupted between the two neighbouring countries, Herzog and his crew became embroiled in the conflict. Rumours spread that Herzog was exploiting the land, smuggling drugs and arms, and planning to kill the locals by 'removing, cooking and eating their grease' (*Burden of Dreams*).

To make matters worse, two agitators from West Germany's Society for Endangered People turned up and began distributing photographs of pits littered with corpses from Auschwitz, telling the locals that this could happen to them if Herzog was allowed to keep filming. Death threats ensued. Fearing for their lives, Herzog and the crew fled their campsite in late November, waving white flags as they left. It was burned to the ground shortly afterwards.

December 1979
Eight months expunged, as if I wished they had never happened. A year of catastrophes …
Werner Herzog, Conquest of the Useless, *2010*

A year later, Herzog found a new location for filming, but after nearly half of the movie had been successfully shot the leading actor was struck down with amoebic dysentery. Robards was flown home and forbidden by his doctor to return. With filming put back, Mick Jagger dropped out too and Herzog was forced to start his film again from scratch. In desperation, he considered playing the role himself but knew he couldn't pull it off. There was only one man who could: Klaus Kinski.

Herzog had avoided asking him in the first place for good reason: Kinski was notorious for his unpredictable behaviour and tantrums. Wherever there was Kinski, there were fireworks. While previously filming together in the Amazon, tensions got so bad that Kinski threatened to abandon the film. Herzog's response was to put a gun to Kinski's head and threaten to shoot the actor and himself if he quit. The film did get finished, but not before Kinski had taken his own potshots at three of the crew, wounding one. Herzog was deeply aware that the isolation of the jungle could make Kinski 'go bonkers again'. But he asked him anyway.

AFTER REFILMING the first half of *Fitzcarraldo*, Herzog hired several hundred Asháninka – indigenous people living in the rainforests of Peru and Brazil – for the big 'lugging the steamship over the hill' scenes. Having found that the closest hill between two rivers was some 1,000 miles (1,600 km) from civilization, Herzog took Kinski, his filming crew and extras deep into an isolated part of the jungle. Disasters ensued. One of the Asháninka died from drowning; another contracted a fatal illness and passed away overnight. Shortly after, a plane containing five crew members crashed, leaving one paralysed and others critically ill. And, of course, it wasn't long before Kinski began to 'go bonkers', having violent outbursts and tantrums on a daily basis – yelling, screaming and seriously freaking out the Asháninka. But all of this was a mere side dish of calamities to the main course of hellish disasters. Herzog was about to meet the real nemesis of his journey – Mother Nature.

17 April 1981
Today I found my thoughts often dwelling on home, though I am not sure anymore where and what home is. Has bad luck taken refuge with us?
Herzog, Conquest of the Useless

When finally ready to film his big boat scenes, Herzog bought himself two similar-looking steamboats – one for filming on the river, the other for dragging over the hill. Already the isolation of their camp and Kinski's daily, violent outbursts had led many of the crew to question why the director couldn't have done all of the filming just outside of Iquitos rather than 1,000 miles from civilization. Herzog held firm to his belief that the isolation would bring out 'unique' qualities in the actors.

26 April 1981
My shoes are rotting away under me. My underwear keeps disappearing.
Herzog, Conquest of the Useless

After the worst rainy season in decades, the Amazon was now experiencing its worst drought in 65 years. Water levels were so low that Herzog's steamboat chosen for all the river scenes became lodged in a sandbank. Any plans for filming on the water were abandoned until the rains returned and the river rose. Meanwhile, hostilities with a neighbouring community had left three of the Asháninka badly wounded from arrow attacks, one receiving a near-fatal arrow in his neck.

4 May 1981
A day I would rather forget. Kinski had a tantrum. I threw away my shoes.
Herzog, Conquest of the Useless

Work began for the Asháninka to cut a path uphill and across a mile of thick forest, for the second steamboat to be pulled up. As if manifesting the wayward spirit of Kinski, Herzog's only bulldozer proved to be temperamental and unpredictable and frequently broke down. Without it, the film was lost. Fuel had to be flown in by plane and ferried a week up river by canoes. Spare parts needed to be flown in from Miami. Often, they were the wrong parts. Muddy and wet, the terrain was unstable and slippery. There were frequent landslides. In the battle between Herzog and Mother Nature, it was obvious who was winning.

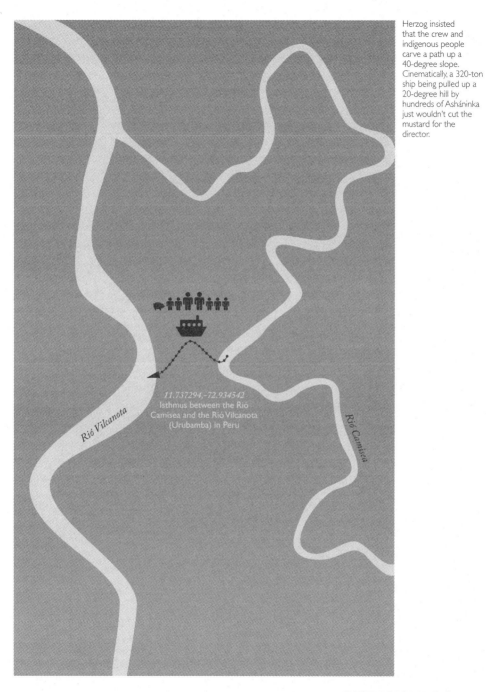

Herzog insisted that the crew and indigenous people carve a path up a 40-degree slope. Cinematically, a 320-ton ship being pulled up a 20-degree hill by hundreds of Asháninka just wouldn't cut the mustard for the director.

11.737294,–72.934542
Isthmus between the Río Camisea and the Río Vilcanota (Urubamba) in Peru

Rió Vilcanota

Rió Camisea

23 May 1981
It becomes clear that no-one is on my side any more, not a single person. None.
Herzog, Conquest of the Useless

As the days and weeks rolled by, Herzog was getting more and more desperate to move the second boat uphill but everything had ground to a standstill. The Asháninka, who had signed up for three months' filming, had now been with them for six months. They were growing restless, and sanitation on the camp was breaking down. A Dominican padre turned up to inspect the quality of life for the indigenous people on Herzog's camp and urged him to find prostitutes for the men. Herzog did as he was told.

A few days later Laplace Martin quit the film. The Brazilian engineer was crucial because of his role in overseeing the construction of the necessary systems to enable the Asháninka to haul the steamboat over the hill. Martin believed that the slope was unnecessarily and dangerously steep and would lead to fatalities. Herzog insisted that the slope remain at 40 degrees. Cinematically, a 320-ton ship being pulled up a 20-degree hill by hundreds of Asháninka just wouldn't cut the mustard for the director. For Martin, the boat had become a '*monstruo*… a monster'. Herzog was later to remark, 'I could tell in his eyes that I was a lost soul.'

More landslides followed. The crew urged Herzog to re-write the script. 'They wanted to protect me from my own insanity,' he wrote in his diary on 5 June. Stranded for several months in a jungle with two steamboats that wouldn't move, there were the inevitable mutterings of a mutiny.

6 June 1981
At night I am even lonelier than during the day.
Herzog, Conquest of the Useless

An attempt to pull the steamboat uphill saw the colossal vessel moving a few feet before a cable snapped and it sank back into the water. Herzog requested stronger cables to be sent from Lima but they never arrived. That same day a woodsman felling trees 20 minutes' walk from the camp and its medical supplies was bitten in the ankle by a deadly snake. Knowing the poison would kill him in less than eight minutes, he was left no option but to remove his own foot with a chainsaw.

For Herzog, it wasn't the 'cursed' boat that was behind all these disasters and suffering but the jungle. In a scene from *Burden of Dreams*, Herzog stands alone in the jungle. His body language is that of suppressed anger and desperation; his words are unequivocal:

'Nature here is vile and base. I see fornication, asphyxiation, choking, the fight for survival. The trees are in misery, the birds are in misery, they don't sing they just screech in pain. It's like a curse weighing on the landscape and whoever goes too deep into this has his share of that curse. So we are cursed with what we are doing here.'

Meanwhile, back at camp, Kinski's tantrums had become so intense and unpleasant that the chief of the Asháninka took Herzog to one side and offered to kill the protagonist. 'Not now,' Herzog replied. The next day he sent the fractious actor away for a week, unsure whether his ambiguous words to the chief might have insinuated that the following day would be a more propitious time to murder his lead actor.

By the end of June the boat was finally moving up the slope thanks to new cables, and even reached the top of the hill. But the curse was yet to be lifted. Water levels in both rivers were still so low that the vessel remained stranded at the summit. The crew would have to wait until the next rainy season before it could be lowered down the other side into the water. Month followed month as the driest season in Ecuador's history unfolded. One steamboat remained wedged in its sandbank, the other was marooned at the top of the hill, like Noah's Ark after the waters of the Flood had subsided. The boats were stuck, the film was stuck, Herzog was stuck. As the months passed, a family with five children and two pigs took up temporary residence in the 'ark'.

27 October 1981
The rain is cowardly.
Herzog, Conquest of the Useless

By November, Herzog was numb, a broken man. 'Today on Wednesday the 4th of November,' he wrote, 'we got the ship from the Río Camisea over a mountain into the Río Urubamba. All that is to be reported is this: I took part. The ship meant nothing to me. There was no pain, no joy, no excitement, no relief, not happiness, no sound, not even a deep breath. All I grasped was a profound uselessness.'

HERZOG'S OWN journey ultimately proved to be far more epic, heroic and tragic than that of Fitzcarraldo's protagonist. In moving a mountain to make a film, he was awarded best director at Cannes Film Festival in 1982. *Fitzcarraldo* itself received mixed reviews, and over the decades that followed Herzog focused most of his film-making on making documentaries rather than fiction.

As Fitzcarraldo's behind-the-scenes horror stories began to filter into the media – together with the release of the documentary about the filming, *Burden of Dreams* – some couldn't help but see the dragging of a steamboat over a hill, inch

Herzog wanted to capture the desperation and sheer willpower of his protagonist. He was never going to use a model for the big scene, preferring to drag a 320-ton steamboat through a mile of impenetrable jungle.

by painful inch, as a perfect metaphor for film-making, at least for Herzog's own uncompromising approach to the art. Others would inevitably compare Herzog to Fitzcarraldo, citing both as fanatics who had exploited the local people of the Amazon for their own gains. But perhaps it is only in looking at the differences between Herzog and Fitzcarraldo that something more revealing can be found.

In Herzog's story of Fitzcarraldo, the natives, afraid that they are tampering with the laws of the jungle, release the steamboat downriver, to avoid being cursed. Fitzcarraldo abandons his missions and admits defeat. But with defeat comes some kind of resolution. He settles on a scaled-down version of his operatic dream, and the film ends with him atop his steamboat, radiant and joyful, surrounded by musicians sharing their divine music with the jungle. Mother Nature has been appeased.

Herzog, too, faced the brute force of nature head on, by attempting in real life to get the steamboat over a hill. Unlike Fitzcarraldo, he finally won out through stubbornness and perseverance; his mission was accomplished. But the victory was superficial. Despite a proclamation that he would 'live or end his life with this project' (*Burden of Dreams*), Herzog did neither. He may have won a physical battle against nature but emotionally he surrendered, coming to berate her as 'vile and base'.

Klaus Kinski was prone to wild outbursts and tantrums; he had already taken potshots at three of the crew. Herzog was deeply aware that the isolation of the jungle could make Kinski 'go bonkers again'.

Like Coleridge's beleaguered 'ancient mariner', the director had brought a curse upon himself – an albatross of monumental proportions; totem became malediction. For Herzog, there was no happy ending, only a sense of 'profound uselessness'. In challenging Mother Nature he had invoked her wrath. The superstitious natives in his own fictional story, it seems, had been right all along. *DB*

SEEKER'S DIRECTORY

Film
Fitzcarraldo (dir. Werner Hertzog, 1982)
Werner Herzog's classic about an Irish adventurer determined to transport a steamship over a mountain deep in the Amazon.

Burden of Dreams (dir. Les Blank, 1984)
Documentary about the chaotic production of *Fitzcarraldo* (1982), blighted by flood, drought and a war between Ecuador and Peru.

The skeletal remains of Herzog's 'cursed' steamer used in *Fitzcarraldo*, steadily being taken over by nature in the Madre de Dios Region of the Amazon.

Book

Conquest of the Useless: Reflections from the Making of Fitzcarraldo, Werner Herzog (Ecco, 2010, reprint edition)

The cinematic master grumbles his way through his diarized account of the making of this monumental motion picture.

Radio

'Grayson on his Bike', BBC Radio 4, 2010

Turner Prize-winning artist Grayson Perry takes his teddy bear across Bavaria on an elaborately decorated Kenilworth AM1 motorcycle.

Field trip

The Moon Museum (1969) by various artists, The Museum of Modern Art, New York.

You'll need to put in a request to see one of 40 existing lithographs of the first artwork to have travelled to the moon, including Andy Warhol's penis doodle.

Strange cargo

*Reg Spiers: the Australian athlete who stowed away in a crate |
Brian Robson: the 'ten-pound Pom' who changed his mind about
emigrating and decided to follow Spiers's example*

One of the stranger tracks to be found among the clattering, shimmering brilliance of
The Velvet Underground's back catalogue is an eight-and-a-half-minute short story
called 'The Gift'. Penned by Lou Reed, 'The Gift' is narrated by the soft Welsh tones
of the band's violinist, John Cale, and juxtaposed with the early Velvet's trademark
thumping beat, guitars and feedback.

Reed originally wrote the story during the early 1960s while attending Syracuse
University in New York. At the time *Alfred Hitchcock Presents* was a popular TV series
and its macabre tales may have played a role in inspiring the young Reed to pen a
story involving a dark twist of fate. 'The Gift' recounts the adventures of Waldo Jeffers,
a lovesick student back home in Locust, Pennsylvania during the summer holidays.
With his college sweetheart, Marsha Bronson, living in Wisconsin, Jeffers has to
endure the pains of a long-distance love affair while also growing anxious about his
girlfriend's fidelity.

Surrendering to a growing paranoia that Bronson might not stay faithful to him –
but without the necessary funds to travel to Wisconsin – Jeffers hatches a plan to have
himself delivered in a large cardboard box to Bronson's house, as a surprise. When he
arrives three days later, Bronson and her friend Sheila attempt to open the mysterious
box but, finding it tightly sealed, resort to using a metal cutter. Unhappily for Waldo,
his head is split open like a melon.

Reg Spiers 1941–

Around the time that Reed was penning the macabre track, Reg Spiers, a 22-year-old
Australian athlete stranded in the UK, had struck upon a similar plan for dodging his
travel fare back to Oz. Spiers, a promising javelin thrower, had come to England in

1964 to train as a potential Olympic contender, but after his wallet was stolen from his apartment he found he didn't have the necessary funds to get home to Adelaide. His young daughter's birthday was fast approaching and he wanted to be there to celebrate it with her.

Spiers had, however, taken some part-time work at an airport in the UK and learned that it was possible to send crates long-distance, marked 'cash-on-delivery'. With the help of a friendly rival – the British javelin thrower John McSorley – Spiers had a special crate constructed, measuring 5 by 3 by 2½ feet (1.5 x 1 x 0.75 m), into which he could stow away during the long journey. Inside the crate, Spiers was able to sit cross-legged or lie on his back with his knees bent. Specially placed handles meant that he could open the crate from the inside. Travelling light, his minimal luggage included tins of food, water, a blanket, a pillow, chocolate, his passport and a large empty bottle in which to empty his bladder.

For five days before the illicit excursion, Spiers ate very little in order to slow down his bodily functions. Then, on 17 October, he had himself transported to Heathrow Airport. His crate claimed to contain tins of paint and had a fictitious Australian address labelled on the side.

SPIERS'S JOURNEY didn't get off to a propitious start: severe fog at Heathrow left him stranded in the baggage hold for 24 hours but, once air-bound, he used the interior handles to leave the confines of his tiny prison cell and stretch his limbs.

REG SPIERS'S CRATE

0.9 m

0.78 m

1.5 m

***DON'T** *mail yourself anywhere*

The first leg of the flight was short, as the plane stopped in Paris to pick up more passengers. At this point, Spiers almost gave the game away. Having been standing in the hold when the plane began its rapid decent, Spiers scurried back into his crate, forgetting that he'd left his urine bottle perched on top. To his relief, on landing, he overheard a conversation between the French baggage handlers that suggested they thought his yellow bottle had been left as a joke by the British baggage handlers: British toilet humour at its most literal.

After being airborne for another ten hours, Spiers landed in Mumbai and was deposited upside-down on the airport's runway in the sweltering Indian heat. This was the most dangerous portion of his journey. Dehydration began to set in and he stripped naked in an attempt to cool himself down, knowing he'd have even more explaining to do if the airport staff heard him and opened the crate to find a parched and naked Australian inside.

From Mumbai, the rest of the journey went relatively smoothly. After a fuel-stop in Singapore, Spiers finally landed in Perth Airport – chosen for its small size and relatively lax security – where his crate was carried to a freight shed and left. When night fell, Spiers snuck out, found some tools to cut his way out of the airport's fence, and hitch-hiked back home, just in time for his daughter's birthday. The entire journey – all 63 hours and 13,000 miles (20,900 km) of it – had hardly cost him a penny.

Spiers was so pleased with himself, and happy to be reunited with his family, that he forgot the one thing he'd promised to do on his return: to let fellow conspirator John McSorley know that he'd arrived home safely. Back in England, the athlete, aware of the very real risks of Spiers's journey, was getting increasingly anxious that something had happened to his friend. As time passed, McSorley felt he had no choice but to contact the authorities and spill the beans. The press soon tracked Spiers down and, true to the pioneering spirit of the Aussies, he was treated as a national hero. A leading Australian politician sent him a telegram of congratulations and five pounds, describing the daredevil journey as 'a gallant effort by a real Aussie'. With so much good publicity around the escapade, Qantas declined to fine Spiers. His luck, however, was not to last.

Brian Robson

While Spiers was riding high on his new-found fame, somewhere in Australia's dusty Outback, a homesick Welshman was at his wits' end. Earlier that year, yearning for adventure, Brian Robson had signed up to be a 'ten-pound Pom' – a cultural exchange programme initiated after the Second World War to encourage Brits to emigrate to Australia. To avoid this being a mere jolly, those who signed up were given a one-way ticket and had their passports confiscated for two years. Having been given a job as a railway ticket clerk in a one-horse town, Robson quickly came to regret his decision. He was bored and lonely. To him, Australia felt like a prison sentence.

'I wanted to go home about 12 hours after I landed,' Robson confessed decades later in an interview for the podcast *Snap Judgment*. 'There was nothing to do. In the Outback we mainly ate beans out of the tin. And they were cold most of the time. All I could think of was cheddar cheese. And home.'

Within a few weeks Robson tried his luck as a stowaway on a passenger ship to England but seasickness got the better of him. Bilious and miserable, he gave himself up, was dropped off in New Zealand and sent back to Australia. Home and freedom seemed beyond reach until Robson chanced upon Spiers's story in a local newspaper. With typical Aussie nonchalance Spiers talked about his adventure as if there was nothing to it. 'I just got in the thing and went. What was there to be frightened of? It's no different to how I travel now overseas. There's the seat. You sit in it and go,' he boasted to a BBC reporter.

Robson reasoned that his only chance of freedom was to follow suit. With the help of two friends in Melbourne he had a crate constructed and planned to pass it off as a computer being sent to the UK for maintenance (computers were ridiculously heavy and bulky back in those days). He packed a book of Beatles songs to keep himself entertained, as well as some plastic bottles and a large suitcase. Following Spiers's example, Robson's crate was labelled 'cash on delivery' and 'fragile, this way up'. The Brit's crate, however, was smaller than Spiers's and the suitcase made it impossible for him to move. Crucially, there was no easy means for him to get out. Instead, he was secured inside with a rope harness and had a pair of pliers to remove the nails on his arrival.

PROBLEMS BEGAN almost immediately after a short flight from Melbourne to Sydney. Unbeknown to Robson, he was now no longer flying direct to the UK. Having been overfilled with freight, his original plane had transferred some of its cargo to a PanAm flight, bound for America. This extra cargo included Robson, who would now be taking the 'scenic' route back to the UK. What's more, the hold on the new plane was unheated. But there was worse to come. While being loaded onto the PanAm flight, Robson's crate was placed upside down in the baggage hold. For the next 22 hours, Robson was trapped upside down, unable to move and in an ice-cold prison.

With the extreme temperatures, and his head taking the full weight of his body, Robson's joints began to swell. He started to experience severe pain and difficulty breathing. Slipping in and out of consciousness, he hallucinated that the plane was about to crash into the ocean. But even in his most torturous hours, Robson was unwilling to break out of his crate, knowing he'd be deported if discovered on arrival. Australia had really got under his skin.

After many torturous hours of torment and pain, his body creeping towards death, Robson finally felt the plane land and his crate being carried into a freight shed. Fumbling for a torch he managed to turn it on, but, with his limbs barely functioning, the torch fell to the floor and he was unable to retrieve it. This simple error saved his life. The light attracted the attention of a freight handler who, peering into the crate, saw what he thought was a dead body and rushed off to get help. When the crate was prized open, Robson's pallid but blinking face revealed that he was alive. Just. Unable to speak and still struggling to breathe, Robson was carried out in his cramped posture by a medical crew. When they attempted to straighten him up, his body jack-knifed back to its foetal position, as if spring-loaded.

Amid his pain and confusion, the drawl of the customs officers, cops and medical crew made it clear to Robson that he hadn't even made it back on home turf, but was in Los Angeles. Had he travelled 42 hours, covered 8,000 miles (12,800 km) and endured crippling pain only to be deported back to the land of cold beans, dust and boomerangs?

Robson was taken to a prison hospital to convalesce and, once his voice had returned, was interviewed by the FBI, who were initially convinced that he'd been kidnapped or was a Russian spy. As the truth unfolded, his story created a media storm. Unsure what to do with him, the authorities finally decided that Robson's fate

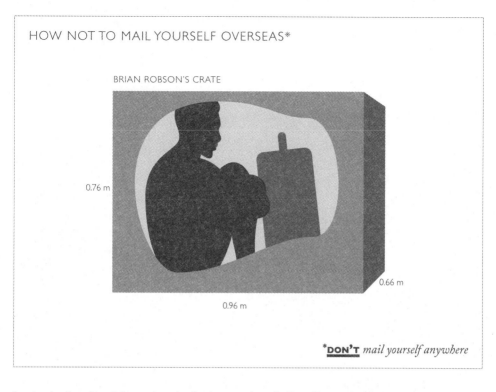

HOW NOT TO MAIL YOURSELF OVERSEAS*

BRIAN ROBSON'S CRATE

0.76 m

0.66 m

0.96 m

*<u>**DON'T**</u> *mail yourself anywhere*

lay in the hands of the airline he had arrived with: PanAm. Like Qantas, PanAm decided to make good use of the publicity and when Robson was well enough, they sent him back to the UK, free of charge. What's more, he flew first class.

HAD ROBSON REMAINED undiscovered in the freight shed in LA and continued the final leg of his journey over the northern ice cap to the UK, the cold would have finished him off for good. By a twist of fate, a lucky accident saved his life. He arrived back in Cardiff to a hero's welcome. And, while the cheddar cheese sandwich that he'd been dreaming of didn't taste quite as good as he'd remembered, he was ecstatic to be home.

Our tale, however, doesn't quite end there. While Robson went on to have a fulfilling life, running a successful chain of retail outlets, Spiers's lot took a very different trajectory. After retiring in the late 1970s, the athlete turned his talents to a different kind of illicit cargo: drug smuggling. In 1981 Spiers was arrested and charged with conspiracy to import cocaine and hashish into Australia. Threatened with a ten-year sentence, he managed to skip bail and carried off another spectacular vanishing act only to be arrested in India the following year, again for drug smuggling.

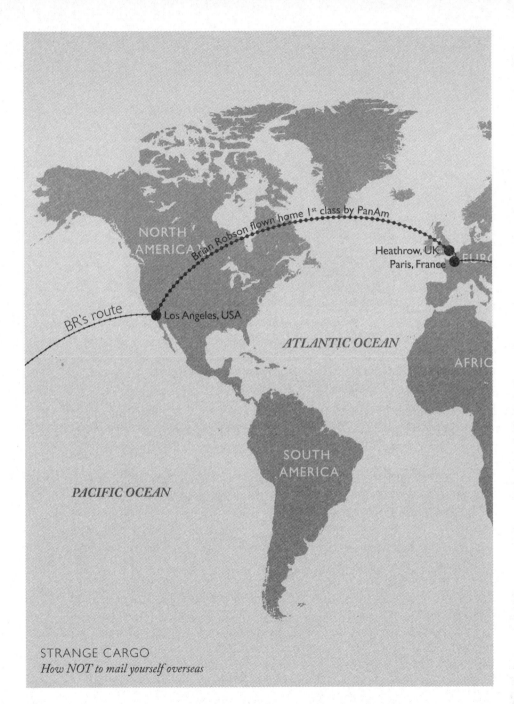

Brian Robson flown home 1st class by PanAm

Heathrow, UK
Paris, France

NORTH AMERICA

EUROPE

BR's route

Los Angeles, USA

ATLANTIC OCEAN

AFRICA

SOUTH AMERICA

PACIFIC OCEAN

STRANGE CARGO
How NOT to mail yourself overseas

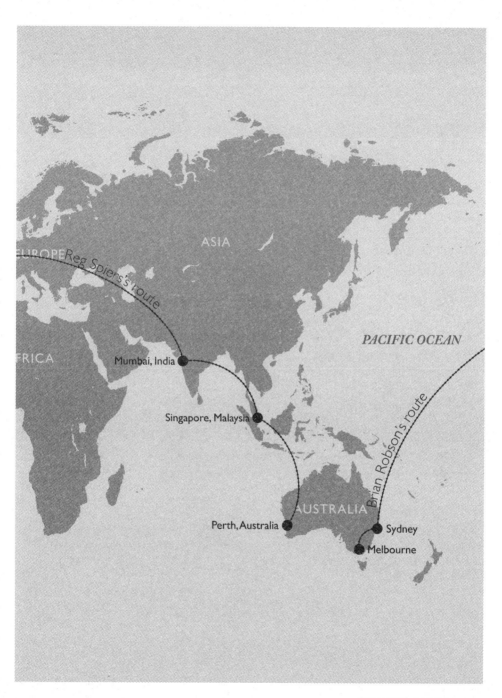

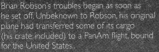
Brian Robson's troubles began as soon as he set off. Unbeknown to Robson, his original plane had transferred some of its cargo (his crate included) to a PanAm flight, bound for the United States.

Once more, Spiers evaded jail and smuggled himself out of the country with a fake passport. The third time he was not so lucky. Caught at a Sri Lankan airport in 1984 with a sizeable quantity of heroin, he was sentenced to death. After a long appeal process, Spiers was finally returned to Australia and in 1987 began a five-year prison sentence in Adelaide.

By the time he reached his forties, Brian Robson had long gotten over his unhappy ordeal in Australia. Having made peace with the country, he decided it was time to return there for a holiday – a chance to see the place with fresh eyes. While it's not recorded whether Robson considered looking up Reg Spiers during his travels Down Under, it must have crossed his mind. The pair had never met and this one-off journey back to Oz would have offered Robson the opportunity to finally meet Spiers in person and to thank him for inspiring his own daredevil escape. And perhaps that's exactly what Robson had planned to do, until he learned of Spiers's incarceration and thought better of it. To witness behind bars the heroic individual who had provided the catalyst for his own break for freedom would have been too much of a dark twist of fate. *DB*

SEEKER'S DIRECTORY

Book
Out of the Box: The Highs and Lows of a Champion Smuggler, Julie McSorley and Marcus McSorley (Roaring Forties Press, 2014)
The remarkable true story of Australian athlete Reg Spiers, who stowed himself in a crate in the luggage hold of a plane to get a free ride home in time for his daughter's birthday.

Podcast
'Boxed In' (2017), *Snap Judgment.* Available at http://snapjudgment.org/boxed-in
Includes a rare interview with an older and wiser Brian Robson, who, desperate to get home, came close to death after being stowed upside down in the hold of a plane for 42 hours.

The Road to En-Dor

E. H. Jones and C. W. Hill: the prisoners of war
whose escape was aided by spirits

Arranging an international trip today is absurdly easy – five minutes with a credit card and some Internet access will sort out your transport from almost any point on the globe to any other. A century ago things were somewhat more complicated. If you were a prisoner of war in Yozgad (now Yozgat), in a remote region in central Turkey, they were more complex still. For a start, escape was considered impossible. Such was the forbidding terrain that surrounded the camp – hundreds of miles of mountain ranges and desert teeming with roaming bands of armed desperadoes – that a surrounding wall was barely necessary. Indeed, it was considered so implausible that any prisoners might try to make a break for it that the sentries, such as existed, were elderly men who frequently dozed at their posts. On top of that, there was a moral imperative to stay put. If an escape attempt took place, punishment was meted out upon the whole camp, a state of affairs that exposed those who even contemplated getting away to the wrath of their fellow prisoners.

Onto this seemingly infertile ground in which to sow travel plans strode two men – Welshman E. H. Jones and Australian C. W. Hill. Undaunted by the difficulties facing them, they devised what might well be the most convoluted and outlandish means of organizing a trip that has ever been contemplated. Furthermore, their attempt to return to their respective homelands not only brought them to the brink of insanity, it came within a fraction of costing them their lives. Their story, told in a commendably matter-of-fact way by Jones in his best-selling but now largely forgotten book *The Road to En-Dor*, is a lesson in how dedication, courage and a sensational amount of lateral thinking can move mountains (or, in this case, get beyond them).

The tale opens in February 1917, when there was still no end in sight to the Great War. Appropriately enough, the odyssey begins with the arrival of a postcard from far away. It was a rare piece of post for Lieutenant Elias Henry Jones and came from an aunt. She suggested he might while away the long evenings by 'spooking' with a ouija

'On fine days they snoozed at their posts' – a 'gamekeeper' on guard at Yozgad.

The journey began when Lieutenant Elias Henry Jones received a postcard from his aunt. She suggested that he might while away the long evenings by 'spooking' with a ouija board.

board. A fellow officer gave Jones a board that he'd made himself with the customary random arrangement of the letters of the alphabet in a circle around the outside. An Irish medic named O'Farrell was drafted in as a second medium and the Psychical Research Society of Yozgad was established.

Since no spirits deigned to make contact through the board, the blindfolded Jones took the trouble to ease the glass around it himself, having memorized the positions of the letters. After rigorous testing, the lieutenant won over even the most sceptical inmates at Yozgad, courtesy of some prodigious feats of memory and some sly tricks, such as putting two imperceptible nicks in the board on which he could lay his little fingers and thus orient himself. Even O'Farrell had no idea that it was Jones who was moving the glass beneath his fingers rather than some force from beyond the grave.

It was at this point that the Welshman was approached by Moïse, the prison camp's young and unlovable interpreter, whom Jones refers to throughout his book as Pimple. News had reached him of the 'spook board'. 'Can you read the future?' he asked. 'I have some questions.' It was enough to give the lieutenant an outrageous idea:

Hitherto spooking had been merely a jest … But now a serious element was being introduced. If I could do to the Turks what I had succeeded in doing to my fellow-prisoners, if I could make them believers, there was no saying what influence I might not be able to exert over them. It might even open the door to freedom.
E. H. Jones, The Road to En-dor: A True Story of Cunning Wartime Escape, *1919*

Jones confessed his hoaxing to a small coterie of friends so that he could enlist their help with his scheme and began the task of reeling in Kiazim Bey, the commandant of Yozgad, a slippery fish whom the Welshman describes as 'the most nebulous official in Asia'.

Shortly afterwards, one of the prisoners came across a rusty revolver that had been buried by an Armenian who had been butchered in the genocide of his people. This led Jones to stage a theatrical performance in which he faked a trance-like state and, spirit-led, located the (reburied) revolver, which he handed over to Pimple and another Turkish official referred to as 'the Cook'. The lieutenant intimated that he had learned through the ouija board that the murdered Armenian had also buried a substantial fortune belonging to his wife (who had also been killed in the pogrom) and that this too might be found with the help of a spirit with the unlikely name of Spook. The prospect of unearthing a great haul of treasure drew the commandant into Jones' web.

O'Farrell was then moved to another part of the camp and so Jones brought in a new 'spooking partner' – a skilled amateur magician named Cedric Hill who had been involved in faking manifestations for a rival ouija board team at Yozgad. Hill's conjuring skills were to come in very handy over the following months.

THE TWO PRISONERS began a series of arduous séances lasting up to six hours at a time. Jones and Hill both wore blindfolds and thus supposedly had no idea what Spook was saying through the board, so Pimple acted as an enthusiastic scribe. This set-up meant that the camp interpreter imagined that he could keep some of Spook's communications secret from the mediums and use them to his own advantage. Jones and Hill could therefore deliberately plant messages, knowing that Pimple would act on them in the belief that he alone knew about them. On occasions, Spook advised Pimple to set traps for the mediums in order to test them – which, of course, Jones and Hill could avoid, since they themselves had devised the traps.

But while Spook was making Pimple more and more biddable while gradually revealing how the murdered Armenian's treasure might be found, Jones and Hill were working on the other difficulty that escaping from Yozgad presented: the need to protect those prisoners who remained from repercussions. Their plan was to make the commandant complicit in their escape. If they had proof that he had aided them, the lieutenants could threaten to send their evidence to the War Office in Constantinople (modern-day Istanbul) if it looked like the commandant might take out his anger at their escape on their fellow officers.

First, they had Spook demand that his two mediums (Jones and Hill) be held in solitary confinement in a separate part of the camp. Ordinarily, this would be impossible to justify unless they had committed some major infringement of the camp rules. The idea was to get the commandant to impose these conditions on them for no good reason – they could later use this as evidence that he was in on their treasure hunt, the ruse they would use to effect their escape. When the wily commandant refused to do this, Spook told Pimple that Jones and Hill should instead be tried in a public court on the charge of 'obtaining war news by telepathic communications'.

Jones had previously claimed that he had been reading the mind of a Turkish man in Yozgad to discover how the war was going. In reality, he had availed himself of snippets of news via coded messages sent in letters to prisoners from their relatives. This led to a surreal situation wherein the commandant asked Spook for advice on all aspects of a successful trial, including what he should write in his report about it to the Turkish War Office. Spook generously dictated said report, which is still no doubt filed away in the Turkish government archives. The trial went ahead. The two men were duly convicted and sentenced to indefinite solitary confinement in a large empty building separate from the other prisoners. As Jones later put it:

> Then we were marched across to our new prison, the first men in history, so far as we knew, to be sentenced for thought-reading.
> Jones, The Road to En-dor

The two prisoners, revelling in their new-found privacy, arranged a séance in which Spook revealed to Pimple that the murdered Armenian had buried three clues as to the whereabouts of his wife's treasure. The first gave the spot from which to measure, the second the distance and the third the direction. They could be found only by reading the thoughts of three people, to each of whom the Armenian had told the location of one of the clues. Spook declared that success in carrying out the mind-reading depended on a formula involving the square of the distance between his two mediums (Jones and Hill) and the target mind. This would be key to ensuring that the commandant allowed them to travel in search of the three people who knew where the clues were buried.

Over a year after the arrival of the postcard from Jones's aunt, the Welshman hid the first clue on a hillside just outside the camp. The two confederates went into a trance and, together with the commandant, Pimple and the Cook, traipsed out of Yozgad towards the spot, led by a friendly spirit with the unfortunate name of KKK. In order to implicate the commandant further, the two prisoners arranged to take a secret photograph of Jones and the three Turks digging for the clue. Hill made a pinhole camera from a chocolate box and half a foraged lens, and 'borrowed' some illicit film from a fellow prisoner. KKK had stipulated that the group perform the 'treasure-test of the Head-hunting Waas'. This was in order to get them all posed and still enough for the covert photographs to be taken.

There was much excitement as Jones dug up a small tin can. It had a false bottom in which was concealed a Turkish gold lira and a piece of paper bearing Armenian

The commandant, Pimple and Cook, furtively photographed with a pinhole camera when finding the first clue outside the prison.

characters. Hill used his sleight-of-hand skills to take three close-range shots without being detected while Jones made as much noise as possible to drown out the click of the shutter. Had they been discovered, there was a very real chance that the commandant would have had them both executed, which doubtless added an edge to the proceedings. One of the photographs survived the war, capturing the surreal event for posterity.

SO FAR, SO GOOD. But just in case the treasure hunt failed for some reason, the two officers concocted a plan B: simulating an illness that would lead to them being included in a prisoner exchange. 'We fixed, provisionally,' Jones noted, 'on madness.'

At this point, Spook revealed the existence of OOO, the spirit of the murdered Armenian man whose wife's treasure they were seeking. Angered that Turks were trying to get their hands on it, OOO proceeded to do everything in his power to disrupt matters. This was a useful tool for Jones and Hill because they were then able to blame OOO's interference for the occasions when events beyond their control thwarted their plan. It also led to séances in which Spook and OOO engaged in fisticuffs in the world beyond and battled for control over the ouija board. On such occasions, it was all the mediums could do to contain their laughter.

The treasure-seekers found the second clue – buried by Hill 4 miles (6.5 km) away on an excursion with the prisoners' skiing club – in similar fashion to the first. That just left the third clue, whose location was known to a man codenamed AAA. Spook revealed that AAA was a Constantinople businessman whose work frequently took him to other

The 'furious' – Welshman
E. H. Jones.

The 'melancholic' –
Australian C. W. Hill.

parts of Turkey. In order for Spook to read his thoughts, the mediums, of course, would have to be moved close to wherever he was. The prisoners' preferred option was the Mediterranean coast. From there they could steal a boat and sail it to Egypt. For good measure, they devised a madcap plan to kidnap as many Turkish soldiers as they could, taking them with them in the boat after somehow drugging them with morphia.

There followed several adventures, one of which included an apparent attempt by OOO to kill the mediums by throwing them down the stairs of their prison and setting off an explosion (Hill's conjuring tricks again). By this time, the commandant was so beholden to Spook – who demanded compliance to his wishes in return for his work on locating the treasure – that the spirit had taken virtual charge of the running of the camp. Its inmates benefitted in improvements to their living conditions; the granting of various privileges such as the right to take walks and (in winter) skiing in the countryside beyond the camp perimeter; and the curtailment of thefts by guards from parcels sent from home. This makes Jones' and Hill's feat almost certainly unique in the annals of prisoner-of-war escapes. It's all the more extraordinary that it occurred during the First World War in a country where thousands of Allied prisoners died at the hands of their captors.

JONES AND HILL took advice from O'Farrell, their friend and doctor, regarding the symptoms they should fake in order to replicate the early stages of mental illness – their plan B. Jones chose to mimic the actions of someone descending into a manic state, while Hill appeared to close completely in on himself, perpetually seeking out a corner in which to be alone, very rarely speaking and constantly reading a bible. Of course, the problem with acting as if you are mentally ill is that, over time, there's a danger that what has been simulated becomes real. Both men subsequently trod a delicate line between feigning their illness and falling prey to it.

To give the commandant a reasonable excuse for having two of his prisoners sent to Constantinople (on which journey they could be diverted to the coast), Spook came up with a plan to allay any suspicions the Turkish War Office might harbour. It involved requesting permission to transfer the two men to the capital to be checked out by psychiatric specialists on the grounds that their states of mind were having a deleterious effect on the rest of the camp. This conveniently also aided plan B in the event that plan A should fail.

As it happened, plan A was thwarted not by any error of their own but by the actions of a well-meaning (and unnamed) fellow officer who assumed that Jones and Hill would not want to have their minds poked into by a team of psychiatrists. The officer was due to leave in the same party as Jones and Hill as part of a group of prisoners who were being moved from Yozgad to another camp. He therefore made an official objection to the two men's presence on the grounds that they might attempt to escape (being of unsound mind), which would result in the entire party being punished.

The commandant got cold feet about the whole project. Jones and Hill – who had now secretly switched to plan B – were kept back until they could be given 'certificates of lunacy' by local doctors before being sent under armed guard to Constantinople. The two prisoners assured the Commandant that Spook would be able to convince anyone who examined them that they were 'mad' by putting them in a trance and controlling them whenever a doctor was about. Thus, he would not get into trouble with the authorities by sending them a couple of malingerers. The important thing was getting to the Turkish capital and staying there for long enough so that Spook could read the mind of AAA and discover where the treasure was hidden.

The local doctors duly diagnosed the Bible-reading Hill as a 'melancholic' and Jones as a 'furious' (according to Pimple's idiosyncratic translation). Jones' most prominent delusion was that everyone who was English was intent on killing him. He wrote his rambling and largely incomprehensible thoughts on the matter in a manuscript entitled *The History of my Persecution by the English*, which eventually filled over 30 large notebooks. The two men had put themselves on a starvation diet, had made their room into a pit of filth and ordure, and had both acted their parts so convincingly that the doctors were terrified of them and were only too pleased to get rid of them by certifying them as mad.

AT 10am on 26 April 1918, Jones and Hill, Pimple, the Cook and half a dozen guards left Yozgad on their 400-mile (644-km) journey to Constantinople. They were to be conveyed to the railhead at Angora on two carts, each drawn by a pair of horses. It took them three days to reach the small town of Mardeen where Jones, acting out his madness (but also driven by compassion), threw money towards fellow victims of the war: groups of starving Turkish children searching for food among piles of litter.

The party lodged at a caravanserai (a roadside inn), and it was there that Jones and Hill took a spectacular risk. Their friend Dr O'Farrell had joked that the best way to convince the Berlin-trained psychiatrists in Constantinople of their madness was for one of them to commit suicide en route. Never less than thorough, they decided that they should both feign an attempt at suicide. Spook had duly informed Pimple that they were going to hang themselves at the caravanserai and that, as soon as he saw the candle go out in their room, he should rush in and save them. Unfortunately, when it came to it, the camp interpreter did not notice the light being extinguished. The following 90 seconds were predictably unpleasant. Jones writes:

> To anyone desirous of quitting this mortal coil we can offer one piece of sound advice – don't try strangulation. Than hanging by the neck nothing more agonizing can be imagined. In the hope of finding a comfortable way of placing the noose we had both experimented before leaving Yozgad, but no matter how we placed it we could never bear the pain for more than a fraction of a second.
> *Jones,* The Road to En-dor

When Pimple eventually did notice that the room had gone dark, he charged in and his two wards were saved. This did not stop one unidentified individual from attempting to finish Jones off by wrapping his arms around his waist and throwing all his weight on him. Once it was established that the two were not going to die, the six Turkish guards duly laid into them as they lay on the floor, beating them with rifle butts, whipping them with rope ends and kicking them with wooden-clogged feet.

Battered and with severely damaged throats, the prisoners continued their journey by cart to Angora. There they waited six days for a train to Constantinople, arriving in the capital on 8 May. Jones and Hill achieved a telepathic link with the businessman, enabling Spook to find out that the third and final clue was buried near a wall in the murdered Armenian family's garden, now part of the prison camp back in Yozgad.

Despite their many travails, it was the following five months in Constantinople – mostly spent in Haidar Pasha hospital – that was to prove the most harrowing period of the lieutenants' adventure.

Jones glosses over some of what transpired, merely noting, 'Before I left Haidar Pasha I was to see sights and hear sounds that will never, I fear, leave my memory.' Every night, after the doctors had left, one of the inmates in Jones' ward (often Jones himself) would be 'pounded with blows' by the staff. Hill had it even worse – moved to another

hospital, he was so badly mistreated and so worn down by dysentery that he almost died. He returned to Haidar Pasha a skeleton, having lost 5 stone (32 kg) in weight.

EVENTUALLY, AFTER the most stringent testing by a whole clutch of psychiatrists, including one with an international reputation, Jones and Hill were declared 'mad' and sent to Smyrna to await repatriation. They were put on separate ships bound for Alexandria (which was in British hands). Playing his part to the last, Jones refused to board the first one available because it was carrying Englishmen who, on account of their nationality, would obviously attempt to murder him. Meanwhile, Spook had reassured Pimple that he had controlled the psychiatrists into giving the two exhausted mediums a holiday so that they could return to Constantinople refreshed and ready to find countless treasure for him and his associates. At last, Jones and Hill could relax, knowing that the final part of their journey – from Egypt to their respective homelands – was now a mere formality. It had taken 20 months from the receipt of the postcard from Jones' aunt to travel from the camp at Yozgad to Allied-held territory.

No abbreviated version of this story can do justice to the sheer complexity of the plan Jones and Hill hatched and carried out. The chapter titles alone demonstrate the sheer oddity of the adventure. These include 'Of the Calomel Manifestation and How Kiazim Fell into the Net'; 'Which Introduces OOO and Tells Why Pimple Got his Face Smacked'; and 'In Which the Spook Convicts Moïse of Theft, Converts Him to Honesty, and Promises Omnipotence'. They even cooked up a number of highly original inventions along the way, including a Four Point Cardinal Receiver, which

THE GOOD, THE BAD AND THE SPOOKY
A list of key players who helped (or hindered) our protagonists' heroic escape

NAME	SPIRIT OR HUMAN?	ROLE
Pimple (Moïse)	Human	The prison camp's young and unlovable interpreter; enthusiastic scribe for Spook (see *below*).
Kiazim Bey	Human	The commandant of Yozgad; a slippery fish, known by some as 'the most nebulous official in Asia'.
OOO	Spirit	The alleged spirit of a murdered Armenian man who was trying to protect his wife's buried fortune.
The Cook	Human	A Turkish official who enthusiastically joined the commandant and Pimple in seeking the Armenian treasure.
Spook	Spirit	The chief spirit who communicated to Pimple via mediums Jones and Hill.
Doc O'Farrell	Human	The original ouija board partner to Jones and who later helped Jones and Hill by instructing them in the best ways of faking madness.
KKK	Spirit	A friendly ghost, who led Jones and Hill to clues outside the camp.
AAA	Human	A Constantinople businessman whose mind the POWs needed to read in order to locate the treasure.

they convinced their captors would allow them to find any buried treasure anywhere, and a Telechronistic Ray which preserved 'both the past and the future in the present for anyone who can get into touch with it'.

This was not merely a house of cards built with clever deceptions upon brilliant lies but a whole palace of cards. A single slip would have brought the whole edifice down. That it did not collapse about their ears and that, after the war, Pimple continued to believe in their powers as mediums despite being informed that the whole set-up had been an elaborate fake, is a mark of their brilliance. The fact that they ran a very real risk of summary execution had they been found out is a mark of their extraordinary nerve.

Agonizingly, having gone through all this, by the time they got to Alexandria, the war had ended. As Jones points out a trifle ruefully, 'We had reached British soil perhaps a fortnight ahead of the "healthy" prisoners.'

He ends his account with the poignant but characteristically uplifting conversation he had with his partner-in-crime when they were reunited in Egypt. The two men, ever modest, reflected not on their achievement but on the help they had received from the small group of pals who were in on their ruse and who assisted them where possible:

We shook hands.
'We've been through a good deal, old chap, and for very little,' I said, with a smile.
…

'For me,' I said gently, 'our hardships have been worthwhile. I have found many treasures.'

Hill understood.

'We have indeed been blessed in our friends,' he said.

Jones, The Road to En-dor

DW

SEEKER'S DIRECTORY

Book

The Road to En-dor: A True Story of Cunning Wartime Escape, E. H. Jones (Hesperus Press, 2014)
The thrilling autobiographical account of a pair of First World War prisoners of war who rely on their use of magic tricks and deception to escape from a Turkish prison camp in 1917. The 2014 edition has a forward from Neil Gaiman, who became utterly captivated by the story aged ten.

Four-Fifty Miles to Freedom (Capt. M. A. B. Johnston and Capt. K. D. Yearsley (Forgotten Books, 2018)
An account of a much more conventional, but still pretty extraordinary, escape from the very same camp. Jones and Hill actually managed to aid these escapers during their own adventure.

Film

'The Road to Endor'
A film with the working title 'The Road to Endor', written by Neil Gaiman and Penn Jillette and produced by E. H. Jones's granddaughter, Hilary Bevan Jones, has been in development since 2008.

Detours of the dead

Gram Parsons: the country singer's cadaver that took an unexpected road trip |
John Joe 'Ash' Amador: the posthumous travels of a death-row prisoner | John
Hunter and Charles Byrne: the battle of wills between an Irish giant and a royal
surgeon | Eva Peron: the bizarre journey of Evita's mummified corpse

To the secular mindset, when you're dead, you're dead; we all convert to worm food.
Our final journey is a corporeal one, from the morgue to the grave. To our animistic
ancestors, however, death was just the beginning – the start of a new odyssey that
might even require the body in its physical form as well as the soul.

As a way of coming to terms with the loss of a loved one, Torajan families in
Indonesia still keep the body at home: preserving, washing and changing its clothes,
sometimes for years after death. After the body is buried, they practise *ma'nene*, in
which they exhume, groom and clean their relative; they even have their pictures taken
with them and walk them around the village to update them on all the changes since
their death. Similarly, every seven years the Madagascan Malagasy lovingly clean and
rewrap the bodies of their loved ones and take them on a dance around the grave. This
ritual goes on until they are fully skeletonized, at which point they may enter heaven.

The concept of a celestial home for the dead is most commonly associated with the
Judaeo-Christian and Islamic faiths. In Scandinavian folklore, all the dead went to
'hell': an underworld ruled by the fearsome giantess Hel. For the ancient Babylonians,
to reach the netherworld of the deceased required a journey through seven gates. At
each gate, an article of clothing had to be removed until the naked dead reached their
gloomy new home – said to be about as fun as a wet weekend in Bridlington.

The ancient Egyptians and Greeks also saw the land of the dead as a miserable
underworld to which the deceased were transported across five rivers. Into the
mouth of the dearly departed, families would place a single coin to pay Charon the
ferryman, who took souls to the realm of Hades. Those who turned up empty-handed
were destined to walk the banks of the Cocytus for eternity; it paid to be on good
terms with the relatives. The Cocytus was one of five rivers said to encircle Hades.

On crossing the Lethe, the dead would lose all memory of their previous lives. After the final river, the Styx, they faced three judges. A merciful judgement led them to a carefree life in the Elysian Fields; a bad judgement meant eternity in Hades.

Of all the myths and traditions that exist around journeys of the dead, however, it is perhaps the Tibetan Buddhists who go into the most detail about the ordeals that await the deceased. After death, a person's spirit is believed to enter bardo, a liminal space in which the deceased must wander for 45 days. Where possible, the dead remain in their own homes for a few days, during which time a monk reads from the *Book of the Dead*, preparing them verbally for the journey ahead. After three days, the consciousness of the deceased will 'awaken' and encounter random images from his or her former life. On seeing a white light, they are discouraged by the monk from approaching; it is there to tempt them back to the transient pleasures of physical existence. To Buddhists, being reborn is no good thing: it means re-entering a world of suffering; it's much better to attain Nirvana and total annihilation.

While the facts of what happens to us after death remain unknowable, many of us harbour intentions around our final resting place. With the support of family and friends, most of us will be granted our final wishes. But even after death there can be obstacles, diversions and – on occasion – thefts that send cadavers on the most unexpected of journeys.

Gram Parsons 1943–1976

In the early 1970s country singer Gram Parsons and Phil Kaufman – his road manager and housemate – attended the funeral of Clarence White. Former guitarist for The Byrds, White had been killed in a road accident by a drunk driver. The overblown ceremony, drenched in Catholic rhetoric, was at odds with what White's friends knew the musician would have wanted. Parsons and Kaufman – high on booze and pills – began to talk about how they'd prefer their own funerals to be. 'Just take me out to the desert, have a few beers and burn me,' Parsons said to Kaufman. The pair made a pact: if ever it came to it, that's exactly what Kaufman would do.

Those inclined to skip past the Country Rock section of their local record store may be unfamiliar with the rock legend that is Gram Parsons. Pioneering a new sound in the 1960s, which fused country music with rock, Parsons recorded seminal albums with his band The Flying Burrito Brothers, played guitar with The Byrds (influencing their *Sweetheart of the Rodeo* album) and released two lauded solo albums, which helped launch the career of Emmylou Harris. Parsons was intrinsic to a musical revolution that exploded out of America in the 1960s and 1970s. Like too many of his generation, he didn't make it to 30.

In the late summer of 1973, having finished what would be his swansong, *Grievous*

Angel, Parsons travelled to the Joshua Tree Inn in the Mojave Desert to kick back and party with friends: his ex Margaret Fisher, heiress Dale McElroy and her boyfriend, Michael Martin. They were planning to get loaded. For some years Parsons's life had been spiralling out of control from drug addiction. Some attribute his self-destructive habits to having an alcoholic father and troubled family life (his father committed suicide when Parsons was 12); for others, it was just another case of rock 'n' roll excess. Having Keith Richards as a friend really can't have helped.

The four checked into Room 8 of Joshua Tree Inn on the early afternoon of September 18 and the partying began. By nightfall Parsons was so far gone that his body shut down. His ex, all too familiar with the effects of a heroin overdose, knew that she had to do something drastic to kick-start Parsons's failing organs and promptly shoved three ice cubes up his rectum to shock his body back into life. By some miracle Parsons came to, even managing to make a joke about his predicament. A few hours later he lost consciousness again. This time he was not so lucky. McElroy attempted to give him mouth-to-mouth resuscitation but to no avail. A comatose Parsons was taken to High Desert Memorial Hospital where he died.

PARSONS'S ROAD MANAGER, Phil Kaufman, was a bearded, heavy-boozing Harley-riding hulk of a man, whose lifelong bladder problems would be immortalized in the Frank Zappa song 'Why Does It Hurt When I Pee?'. In the early 1960s Kaufman got by as an actor, until a drug bust left him sharing a prison cell with the notorious cult leader Charles Manson. After leaving prison, Kaufman became a roadie and got his first job as driver to The Rolling Stones then later with Parsons's band, The Flying Burrito Brothers. Kaufman initially didn't take to Parsons, whom he took as a privileged, ill-mannered Country obsessive, but the pair eventually became close friends and were living together at the time of Parsons's untimely demise.

Fiercely loyal to those he loved, when Kaufman heard of Parsons's death, he drove straight from Los Angeles to the Joshua Tree Inn, cleaned away all incriminating evidence of the drug-fuelled party and buried the remaining stash in the desert. Next he called the morgue to enquire about Parsons's body and discovered, to his dismay, that it was at LA airport.

At Parsons's stepfather's request, the cadaver was bound for a Continental Airlines flight back to the family home in New Orleans. Kaufman knew that there was no love lost between Parsons and his stepfather – who he often referred to as a 'pinky-ring alligator-shoe asshole' – and he had not forgotten the funeral pact made with his buddy.

Kaufman and Parsons's friend Martin loaded up on alcohol and borrowed a hearse – bought by a friend for camping trips – and, for reasons never fully explained, donned rhinestone jackets and cowboy hats. Despite their boozy breaths and unlikely

Joshua Tree Inn is a site of pilgrimage for Gram Parsons fans. Room 8, where the country-music legend died of an overdose on 19 September 1973, is still the most popular.

attire, the pair passed themselves off as mortuary workers at the airport and the ever-persuasive Kaufman convinced staff that he had orders from Parsons's family to ship the body to a different airport. When a cop car turned up and inadvertently blocked their exit, Kaufman brazenly asked the driver if he'd help get Parsons' body into the back of the hearse. The cop obliged and they drove off unhindered, despite drunkenly bashing into the hangar door on the way out.

Accounts differ as to how loaded Martin and Kaufman actually were by the time they reached Joshua Tree. Kaufman likes to describe their state as 'functioning drunks' but also admitted that they reached a point where they felt 'unable' to drive any further and, at 1am, pulled over at a spot known as Cap Rock.

Parsons's casket and 5 gallons of gasoline were removed from the hearse. 'All right Gram, on your way,' Kaufman yelled. He poured gasoline on the corpse, threw on a lit match and Parsons exploded into flames.

While Joshua Tree park laws were, at the time, unclear about DIY cremations, they took their fire ban seriously. The flames from the pyre, visible for miles, soon attracted attention of the park staff and when Kaufman and Martin saw headlights on the horizon, all plans to bury Parsons's charred remains were forgotten. They scarpered, leaving the smouldering cadaver beside the road, and went in search of somewhere safe to pull over and sleep.

Driving back to LA the following morning, Kaufman and Martin were, once again,

Cap Rock, where Kaufman burned Parson's body, has become an unofficial memorial.

Gram~
we adore your music
tilogmed i Norge
♡ sailorjfg

tanked up from a liquid breakfast. Their booze-fuelled driving came to the attention of the police and, when a traffic cop opened the door of the hearse, umpteen bottles and two men dressed as rhinestone cowboys tumbled out. Kaufman and Martin were duly handcuffed to the steering wheel but, while the cop went for backup, Martin's skinny wrists enabled him to slip free and the pair drove off, escaping arrest.

The story of Parsons's unlikely sojourn hit the headlines a few days later, and it was only a matter of time before the police came looking for the likely culprits. As there was no law against body-snatching in California, Kaufman and Martin were only charged with unlawful possession of a casket and 'littering' a national park. Kaufman was, however, served with one year probation. When the judge announced this, Kaufman cheekily replied: 'Does that mean I can't steal a body for another year?', narrowly avoiding a second spell in jail for insubordination.

Parsons's remains were finally returned to New Orleans for a 'proper' funeral but it's to Joshua Tree that his fans make pilgrimages to pay their respects. Room 8 of the Joshua Tree Inn is treated as a shrine, filled with photos and memorabilia, and can still be hired out to visitors. By Cap Rock, an unofficial memorial bears the words: 'Safe At Home'. As far as Parsons's fans are concerned, the true spirit of their idol resides in Joshua Tree. Freed from his addictions and troubled mind, would Parsons really have wished for his body to be doused in petrol for a hasty, drunken roadside funeral? It's a sobering though. As the saying goes: be careful what you wish for.

John Joe 'Ash' Amador 1975-2007

> I did not kill your loved ones. I do not know who did and you know I didn't do it. I wish I could tell you the reason why, or give you some kind of solace. You lost someone you loved very much just as my family are going to lose me in a few minutes and I am sure he died unjustly just like I am. To my family and friends even though I die, that love for you will never die.
> *Luis L. Ramirez, 1963–2005*

These, the last words of death-row prisoner Luis L. Ramirez, are scrawled on the back wall of a terraced house in an unassuming cul-de-sac of West London. The house itself, however, is far from unassuming. A kaleidoscope of colours adorn the front and back in the form of mosaics and political and artistic slogans. A quote from the comedian Bill Hicks runs along the top of one wall. Even the owner's two cars – a truck and a London taxi – have been given a psychedelic makeover with thousands of tiny mosaic tiles.

It is the work of artist Carrie Reichardt who, struggling with her mental health, found salvation in a new hobby: mosaicking. A self-diagnosed obsessive-compulsive,

Exterior of Reichardt's house in West London.

Reichardt rarely does things by halves – the building's exterior took countless months of work.

In 2000 Reichardt responded to an advert in *The Big Issue* entitled: 'Human Writes – could you befriend a man on death row?' She was intrigued and began a correspondence with Luis Ramirez, incarcerated in 1999 in a Texas jail for murder. The pair shared personal stories and details of their lives, their families and their children, forging a deep friendship through five years' worth of letters. They even shared a love of mosaicking.

During this time Reichardt immersed herself in studying the US death penalty and was horrified to discover that nearly all death-row prisoners come from poor areas and ethnic backgrounds. Researching Ramirez's case, Reichardt came to believe – as Ramirez claimed right up until his death – that he had been convicted on the evidence of one man: an unreliable witness and a drug addict. She began to see how easy it was for suspects to be given the death penalty on flimsy evidence and hearsay.

For Reichardt, there was a painful truth in the words of John Spenkelink, the first person to be executed in Florida after the death sentence was reinstated in the state in 1976: 'Capital punishment means those without capital are punished.' As Reichardt bluntly put it herself, 'There are no rich people on death row.' She began campaigning for greater public awareness of the insidious aspects of America's death penalty, and how and why it should be changed.

Back wall of Reichardt's house, dedicated to the memory of Luis Ramirez.

IN 2005 Ramirez's date of execution was set, and he wrote to Reichardt asking if she would visit him during his last two days of life. It wasn't an easy decision to make. Reichardt knew how upsetting the experience would be, but she also had no intention of letting her friend down.

Arriving in Texas, Reichardt drove to a remote wood cabin on the perimeter of a woodland, not far from the prison. The shelter had been set up for the specific purpose of housing the families and friends visiting their loved ones for the last time. The walls and bedroom were decorated with death-row artefacts, newspaper reports and even the photograph of a gurney – the table on which the condemned is given their final lethal injection. It didn't make for a good night's sleep. 'Walking into death row the next morning my knees gave way with fear,' Reichardt recalled, but she was able to fulfil her promise to be with her friend for the final 48 hours of his life.

Once back in the UK, Reichardt threw herself into mosaicking the back of her house, creating a memory wall in Ramirez's honour into which she embedded his prison ID card and inscribed his final statement. Eight months later the work was unveiled, and Ramirez's family flew from Texas to participate in a street party. The ceremony should have bookended a highly emotional affair for Reichardt, had it not been for a letter from Luis Ramirez's girlfriend that she received shortly after.

It turned out that John Joe 'Ash' Amador – another death-row prisoner – lived in the cell directly next to Ramirez's, and Ash happened to be husband to Ramirez's girlfriend's sister. For 12 months following Ramirez's execution, Reichardt and Ash had also corresponded until the day when his execution was announced. The letter asked if Reichardt would be happy to attend Ash's execution, too – to support him and his family, who had all grown close to her. While again wary of her mental wellbeing, Reichardt couldn't refuse. However, after a chance encounter with a man called Nick Reynolds, her second journey to death row was to take a rather different turn.

IN 1977, in response to the Queen's Silver Jubilee celebrations, The Sex Pistols performed songs while sailing up the River Thames in London, until forced to stop by the police. Thirty years on, on 27 June 2007, British Prime Minister Tony Blair was in his last day in office. As a two-finger salute to Blair – and a nod to the anniversary of the Pistols' gig – the punk band Sick Note hired a boat to cruise the Thames and played a noisy set outside of Parliament. Reichardt was invited to join them. Onboard she met Nick Reynolds (son of Bruce Reynolds, the mastermind behind the Great Train Robbery) who had a sideline in creating death masks – plaster-of-Paris casts depicting faces of the deceased. Reynolds's personal collection of death masks included those of William Blake, Napoleon Bonaparte and Ken Russell, while his own commissions included Peter O'Toole and The Sex Pistols' former manager, Malcolm McLaren.

Reichardt and Reynolds hit it off and began sharing stories of their adventures. Reichardt told Reynolds that she had been asked to mosaic a truck as part of an 'art car' parade in Manchester. The commission was to make a 'Tiki Love Truck' with hula girls handing out messages of love to the crowds. With this the pair struck upon an idea: what if – with Ash and his family's blessing – Reynolds were to accompany Reichardt to Texas and make a death mask with Ash to put on her Tiki Love Truck, to keep his memory alive?

Ash and his family did give the idea their full support – with the death mask he would not be just be another forgotten prisoner killed on death row. The pair flew out to Texas, where Reichardt was one of Ash's five chosen witnesses. It was another emotionally charged experience for her:

> I've never had such anxiety in the whole of my life. There we were, packed up in this room, with a small window, overlooking Ash, strapped into the gurney. The main thing I remember is seeing his wife cleaning the condensation from the glass so she could keep eye contact with her husband. The lethal injection is meant to grant prisoners a short, painless death; it took Ash seven and a half minutes to die.
> *Carrie Reichardt in interview with David Bramwell, March 2018*

Reynolds and Reichardt knew that they would not have permission to create the death mask in the prison. They had learned, however, that Texas was the only US state

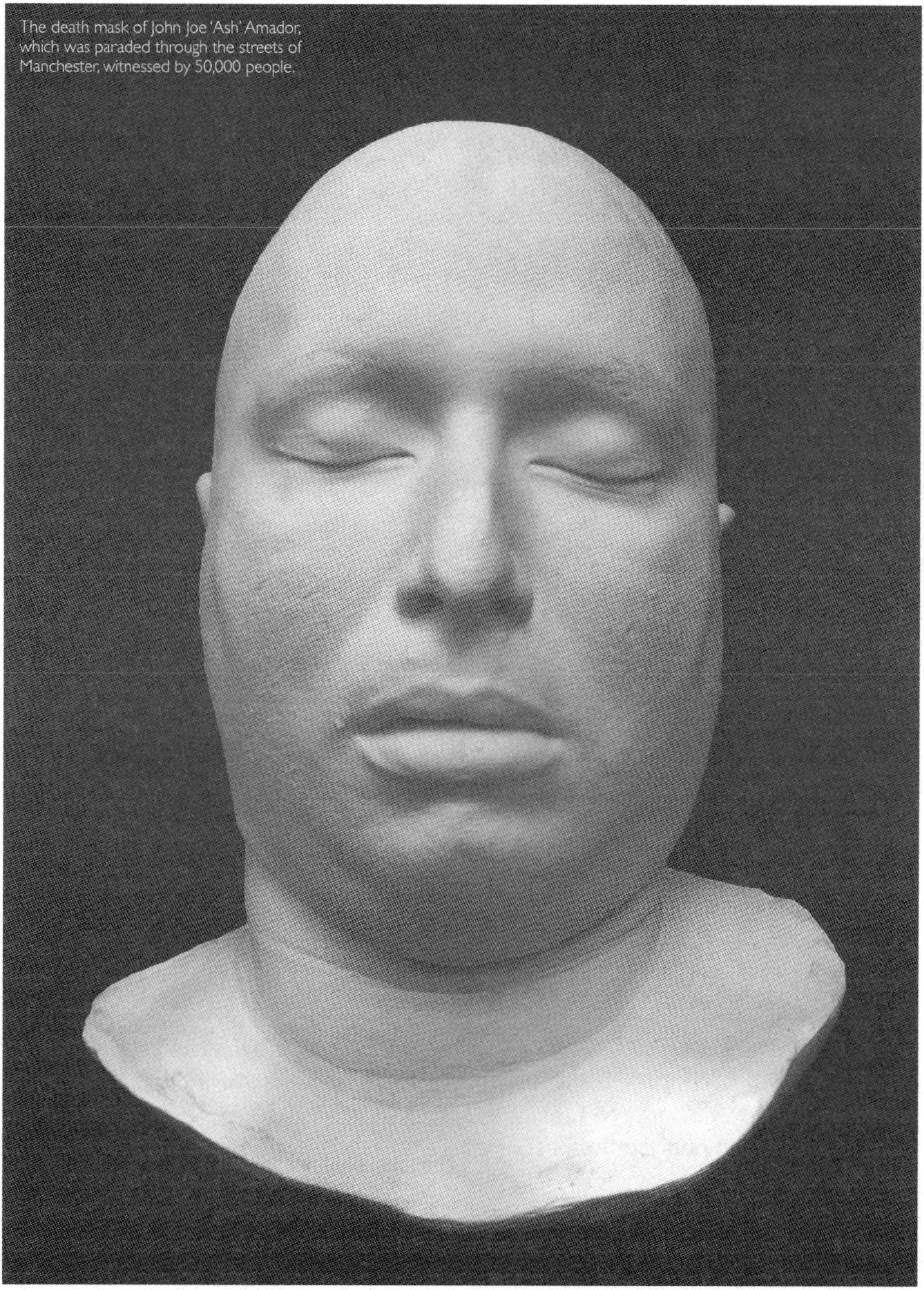
The death mask of John Joe 'Ash' Amador, which was paraded through the streets of Manchester, witnessed by 50,000 people.

Carrie Reichardt's Tiki Love Truck – a mobile mosaic mausoleum – joined a street parade in Manchester on 8 September 2007.

that permitted the family to remove the body in order to take it the morgue, provided they brought their own body bag. The pair had scoured local shops for such an item the previous day, along with a few kilos of plaster of Paris.

Less than an hour after Ash's execution, Reichardt, Reynolds and the deceased's family left the prison with his body in the boot of their car, and headed in the opposite direction from the morgue. They knew what they were about to do was not entirely legal. If pulled over by the cops, they would have had a lot of explaining to do. After half an hour they reached a small cabin Ash's widow had rented. Reynolds removed a door from its frame, placed it across two cabin beds and laid Ash's body on top; it was still warm.

Working in intense heat, Reynolds spent two hours casting Ash's head and the arm that had been chosen for the lethal injection, before embarking on another long drive to take his body to the morgue. Owing to Texas's severe penal laws, the prison had a strictly non-contact policy, even for the final hours before a prisoner's execution. In making the death mask, Reynold's hands on Ash's face marked the first time his body had received intimate contact in 12 years.

Eight days later Reichardt's bright-orange Tiki Love Truck, with Ash's head on the raised roof, took part in the art car parade, witnessed by 50,000 people in Manchester.

Over the next seven years the truck was driven around Blackpool, Glastonbury, various UK festivals and Australia. It even spent six months in London's V&A Museum as part of a show called 'Disobedient Objects'. Ash's head was seen by nearly half a million visitors, encouraging them to engage in conversation about the US death penalty. Just before his death, Ash said to Reichardt:

> I can't believe you came all this way for me. Death masks are usually bestowed on kings. Now I know I'm not trash. I'm somebody.
> *Carrie Reichardt in interview with David Bramwell, March 2018*

Reichardt would later comment:

> Death row dehumanizes. A death mask engages people in a narrative, which re-humanizes them. I believe you can go to the darkest place and find the light. Through art and creativity you can bring something back. It's a unifier. Art gives us our humanity.
> *Carrie Reichardt in interview with David Bramwell, March 2018*

The Tiki Love Truck continues to travel the world. Death-row prisoner John Joe 'Ash' Amador's memory lives on in a journey that has yet to end.

Charlie Chaplin 1889–1977

Unlike Parson's trip to the desert or Ash's death mask, in the majority of cases when a cadaver takes an unplanned journey, it's rarely in the interests of the deceased. In 1978, a few weeks after being buried near his home in Lausanne, Switzerland, Charlie Chaplin's body was stolen by two men. They reburied the coffin in a secret location a mile from the grave and contacted Chaplin's family, demanding £400,000 for the return of his cadaver. After tapping the family phone and keeping a watch on over 200 phone boxes in the area, police finally apprehended the criminals responsible. Chaplin's widow had no intention of paying the ransom whatever the outcome. 'Charlie would have thought the whole thing ridiculous,' she is reported to have said.

Charles Byrne 1761–1783

One man who lived in mortal dread of his body taking an unwelcome journey after death was Charles Byrne, a renowned giant in the Georgian period. Born in Ireland in 1761, the adult Byrne came to stand a towering 7 foot and 7 inches (2.31 m), despite being born to parents of modest height. While Byrne's father jokingly put his son's height down to him being 'conceived on top of a hay stack', it's now known that he suffered from benign tumours in his pituitary gland. Those effected with gigantism tend to live a short life.

Capitalizing on his outlandish appearance, by his late teens Byrne established himself as a novelty act, touring Scotland and the north of England before settling in London. The sensation of Byrne's immense stature, his gentle, convivial manner and his ability to light his pipe from street lamps secured him celebrity status. He even inspired and appeared in a hit stage show, *The Giant's Causeway*, and was name-checked by Dickens in *David Copperfield*.

Byrne earned a good living, dressed well and had an apartment above a cane shop near Trafalgar Square with his own specially made furniture. Visitors could pay to visit him in his residence, adjacent to Cox's Museum, the Victorian equivalent of a Ripley's Believe It or Not!

Despite being relatively well off, Byrne did not lead a happy life. He suffered from tuberculosis and musculoskeletal pains, and – uncomfortable with his celebrity status and being a living spectacle – became an alcoholic. A greater contribution to his drinking, perhaps, was a fear that plagued his every waking hour: what would happen to his body after death? Byrne was a Christian and, according to the 18th-century reading of the Bible, any corpse that had been interfered with might not be accepted into heaven. Unfortunately, Byrne also lived in an era when cadavers for dissection were difficult to obtain for precisely that reason, opening the floodgates to a thriving black market in corpses. Medical men regularly fraternized with 'resurrection men' – grave-robbers. Such was the bounty for a corpse, some even resorted to murder. Byrne knew that to many surgeons – especially George III's surgeon, John Hunter – his body was the jackpot.

A brain tumour took Byrne's life at the age of 22, and within hours a crowd of surgeons had surrounded his house. However, the canny giant had pre-empted the situation, paying friends and fishermen handsomely to ensure that he was buried at sea in a lead-lined coffin. In accordance with his wishes, Byrne's corpse was whisked away to the coast and cast overboard where the coffin sank to the bottom of the North Sea, never to be found. Unfortunately for the Irish giant with a fear of body theft, it was not his corpse that filled the coffin, but rocks.

JOHN HUNTER liked to get his way. A progressive medical man, anatomist and good chum of Erasmus Darwin, Hunter owned a private museum filled with unusual medical specimens. He was also known to fraternize with resurrection men, who would regularly bring corpses to his back door.

Hunter had been so hungry to get his hands on Byrne's corpse that he had paid Byrne's embalmers the equivalent of £30,000 to exchange the body for rocks on its journey from London to the sea. After getting hold of the corpse, the surgeon chopped up the body, boiled the flesh and had a special cabinet made for his new trophy: Byrne's skeleton.

Hunter never publicly exhibited Byrne in his museum during his lifetime, perhaps fearful of a public scandal. Despite his social standing, Hunter's nefarious activities did

Charles Byrne captured in a John Kay etching (1794), alongside giant George Cranstoun and others of shorter stature and average height.

mean that he had his detractors in London society. One such was the author Robert Louis Stephenson who, in basing his novella *Strange Case of Dr Jekyll and Mr Hyde* (1886) on Hunter, turned the tables on the surgeon as a collector of 'freaks' to a freak of nature himself.

London's Hunterian Museum remains a popular attraction. Among its many singular specimens – including Thomas Thurlow, the Bishop of Durham's rectum and Winston Churchill's dentures – stands its prize exhibit – the skeleton of Charles Byrne. Despite campaigns to persuade the museum to bestow upon Byrne the burial at sea he desperately wished for, he remains there to this day, seen by thousands of visitors each week. The Hunterian Museum claims that Byrne's body is still of benefit to the medical profession; critics, however, ask why it can't be replaced with a plastic replica. Held erect by pins, there's an awkwardness in the skeleton's posture, as if it is shrinking away. Two hundred and fifty years on, the gentle giant still can't evade the public gaze he so badly sought refuge from during his short life.

Eva Duarte 1919–1952

The meteoric rise of Eva Duarte, known by many as Evita, from poverty and obscurity to being Argentina's most powerful woman, has been romanticized by a popular musical, yet what happened to her body after death is perhaps the greatest and strangest odyssey a cadaver has ever undertaken.

An illegitimate child from a poor rural family, Eva Duarte ran away to Buenos Aires with a tango singer when she was 15, and found her calling as a model, theatre performer and – later – as a minor film actress and popular radio personality. Never shy of charming or exploiting useful connections, in 1944 she became acquainted with Colonel Juan Perón, a politician on the rise. The pair became lovers and were soon married. When the colonel was elected president two years later, Duarte, still in her twenties, became Argentina's First Lady.

Eva Perón expressed a deep sympathy for the underclass of Argentina – known as the *descamisados*, or 'shirtless ones' – and, after assuming the role of Ministry of Labour and Health, she embarked on a mission to give Argentina's poor better housing and higher wages. Through her own charity, The Eva Perón Foundation, she built new hospitals and orphanages and campaigned for women's suffrage. Such reforms earned her the love of millions, who called her Evita and 'Lady Bountiful'; some went as far as calling her a saint.

Evita's detractors – the bourgeoisie and nobility – dismissed her as a pushy social climber with expensive, unsophisticated tastes. In many ways, the Peróns established a textbook dictatorship: Juan actively repressing all opposition and expressing fascist sympathies; Evita overdoing it on the shoes and Gucci handbags. Yet her desire to

The official 'smiling' portrait of President Juan Domingo Perón, wearing a presidential sash as a symbol of office and accompanied by the First Lady, María Eva Duarte de Perón, popularly known as 'Evita' (1948).

Argentine mourners line the streets of Buenos Aires, covering their heads with newspapers to shelter from the rain and queueing to see the body of First Lady, Eva Perón.

help the country's poverty-stricken seems to have been genuine, so much so that she worked herself into the ground and became seriously ill after only a few years. Her diagnosis with terminal cervical cancer was kept secret from both Evita and the Argentinian people. She died in 1952, aged 33.

Perón's decision to have his wife embalmed just hours after death was as much a political one as sentimental. In this way, Evita could live forever in the hearts of the people who worshipped her and as an immortal work of art. Her body was displayed in the headquarters of the Office of Health and Labour, where she had spent so much of her time. Over the next fortnight, 2 million Argentinians turned up to see, touch and kiss her. Some fainted; seven were killed in a crush.

Eva Perón's tomb,
Cementerio de la Recoleta,
Buenos Aires, Argentina.

For her body to be truly immortalized, however, Evita's body needed to be mummified, a process that would take over a year to complete. At the end of the process she looked like a waxwork doll, less than 5 feet (1.5 m) high. Her cadaver remained in the office while work began on a colossal monument in her honour. Colonel Juan Perón stayed in power, becoming more corrupt, while his libertarian reforms – which included the legalization of prostitution and divorce – outraged many, not least the Catholic Church. Unrest led to a military coup in 1955 and Perón fled into exile.

The new regime kicked back against 'Peronism', making it illegal even to discuss it; those found in possession of a picture of Evita faced serious consequences. As part of the removal of Peronism, the authorities knew it was important to deal with Evita's body, but what to do with it? Destroying her corpse was bad for business – it would make her a martyr – but so was keeping it. It was decided that she would be buried in an unmarked grave, in the largest cemetery in Buenos Aires.

THE JOB WAS left in the not-so-capable hands of Carlos Eugenio Moori Koenig, the head of military intelligence – a man described, by those who knew him, as a 'strange fish'. Somehow Koenig just never got around to completing the task in hand. First he had three 'copies' of Evita's mummified body made. He buried one in an attempt to throw any Peronists off the scent and hid the real body in a warehouse. A fire in the warehouse led to the body being temporarily stored in the back of an army van. Disconcertingly for Koenig, the following morning the van was surrounded by flowers and candles. Evita was transferred to another van and moved to a different part of the city. The next morning, again, flowers and candles surrounded the vehicle.

Spooked, Koenig hid Evita's body behind a cinema screen. Still the flowers and candles appeared. The tributes were undoubtedly the work of Peronist sympathizers within the new regime, but it was deeply troubling for Koenig who had by now developed an obsession with Evita and was beginning to act a little unhinged. Next, he stored the body in a house belonging to one of his men but he too developed an unhealthy attachment to Evita. Hearing a noise in the night, the soldier rushed downstairs to see a figure standing by the corpse. Taking it to be a burglar, he grabbed his pistol and fired, inadvertently killing his own wife.

Koenig retook possession of Evita, hiding her in his attic under a pile of packing boxes marked as electrical equipment. Next, he moved her into his office, standing her upright to show off to visitors. By this point Koenig was believed to be suffering from a nervous breakdown and was relieved of his duties. Instead, the authorities instigated 'Operation Cadaver' and planned to send Evita's corpse off to Europe to be buried in an unmarked grave. To put any loyalists off the scent, and with the covert assistance of the Vatican, decoy coffins with fake Evitas were sent to various Argentinian embassies across Europe.

When the now mad-as-a-box-of-frogs Koenig got wind of this, he set off in pursuit, inadvertently following one of the fake Evitas to Germany, never to be seen again. The real body was taken by boat to Milan where Evita remained buried in a grave under the name María Maggi, undiscovered for 14 years.

THROUGHOUT THE 1960s Argentina remained a divided country with violence and unrest on the increase. As a means of placating the growing voices of dissent, the powers-that-be made Peronism legal again and ordered that Evita's body be sent to the exiled Juan Perón – now living with his third wife, Isabel, in Madrid. When the coffin arrived at Perón's house, Evita was not looking her best. The body had been

One of many plaques on Eva Perón's tomb. The translation reads:

EVA PERON RIP
25 July 1952 – 1982
Do not cry for me neither lost or far away
I am an essential part of your existence
All love and pain were foreseen
I fulfilled my humble echoing of Christ
whose footsteps were followed by
HIS DISCIPLES

Aerial view of La Recoleta Cemetery, Buenos Aires in Argentina – Evita's final resting place in the family tomb.

bashed about, she was missing a finger (removed in the coup of 1955 to verify her true identity), her feet were mangled (possibly from all the time Koenig had her standing up) and her head had nearly separated from her shoulders. But she was back.

Perón placed Evita near the dining-room table in an open casket, making her quite the conversation piece for dinner parties. His wife, Isabel, allegedly slept next to Eva's body on occasion to soak up the 'political magic'.

In 1973 Perón was reinstated as president but died the following year. Evita remained in Madrid, alone in the house. Isabel took over as president and, bowing to public pressure, had Evita's casket brought from Spain to Argentina. After much work to make her look presentable again, Evita went back on public display for a few days, with her husband's corpse next to her. Argentinians came in their hundreds of thousands to see her.

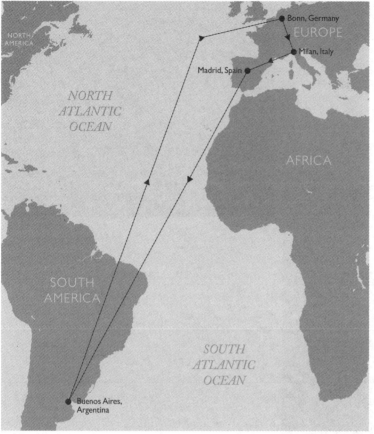

The clandestine travels of Evita's mummified corpse.

In 1976 Isabel was deposed and yet another coup led to one of the darkest and bloodiest times in Argentina's history. To avoid Evita's corpse going on further unwanted excursions, the body was interred in her family mausoleum. Such was the authority's fear of further interference, she was placed 16 feet (5 m) underground in a fortified casket, covered with steel and cement. The crypt itself is said to be able to withstand bombs, fire and even nuclear war.

While still divisive, Peronism remains an integral aspect of Argentina's political landscape and Evita is far from forgotten. For many, her life was like something out of a fairy tale, as was her death. In the late 1970s, with the country plagued by coups, fascist dictatorships and violence, many believed that nothing less than a fairy tale ending could bring their country back to life. Argentina may be a very different country now – more peaceful and more democratic – yet the legacy of Evita endures: the body of its sleeping beauty remains deep in the vaults of an impenetrable fortress. DB

Films
Gram Parsons: Fallen Angel (dir. Gandulf Hennig, 2004).
This documentary, made on location by director Hennig and American music journalist, musician and biographer Sid Griffin, features rare footage of Parsons's performances as well as interviews with friends and devotees, Parsons's wife Gretchen, his sister and daughter, Keith Richards, Emmylou Harris, Chris Hillman and Phil Kaufman.

Grand Theft Parsons (dir. David Caffrey, 2003).
This black tragic comedy, staring Johnny Knoxville as road manager Phil Kaufman, received mixed reviews when it premiered at the 2004 Sundance Film Festival.

Albums
The Gilded Palace of Sin (1969) is the first album by country rock group The Flying Burrito Brothers, fusing folk and country with gospel, soul and psychedelic rock.

Grievous Angel (1973) is the second solo album by Gram Parsons, released four months after his death. It achieved critical acclaim but failed to do much commercially. It was, however, recognized as a successful example of a hybrid between country and rock 'n' roll – or 'Cosmic American Music' as Parsons called it.

Art
Delve into the remarkable outsider art of Carrie Reichardt, including such pieces as *Mary Bamber – a Revolutionary Woman* (2011), a statue of one of the lesser-known activists in the suffrage movement, commissioned to stand on the notorious Speaker's Corner in Liverpool, and *Little Miss DMT*, a mosaic two-headed elephant created for a charity display in Milan. She was originally named 'Bunga Bunga' in reference to the then Italian Prime Minister's alleged sex parties, but the name was considered too politically sensitive for the parade's organisers. **carriereichardt.com**

Field trips
You can still visit Charles Byrne's cadaver at the Hunterian Museum, 35–43 Lincoln's Inn Fields, London WC2A 3PE

Take a pilgrimage to the final burial place of Eva Perón: La Recoleta Cemetery, Buenos Aires, Argentina.

Voyage to the centre of the Earth

Dallas Thompson: the personal trainer who planned to fly into the centre of the Earth | Rodney M. Cluff: the adventurer who mounted an expedition to uncover the world's best-kept secret

Dallas Thompson

Late night, 4 October 2002: an agitated guest appears on a cult American radio show, *Coast to Coast AM*. Dallas Thompson, a 31-year-old former personal trainer from Bakersfield, California, is breathlessly recounting his near-death experience to presenter Art Bell.

Five years earlier, Thompson's car had hydroplaned at 70 miles per hour (113 kph), spinning four times before careering off a 250-foot (76-m) cliff. The fireman who found his blue Honda Accord was astounded that he hadn't been decapitated. 'It was turned into a convertible and that's not a convertible,' Thompson tells the radio presenter excitedly.

Thompson goes on to reveal that the car accident has opened him up to 'now'. 'When you become now, the future is not the future, the future is now,' he explains to a bemused Bell. The experience has also awakened in him a worrying insight: the Earth is about to suffer an electromagnetic shift and we're about to be shaken off. The end of the world is coming 'like a thief in the night', he says; the only way for us to survive is to access the caves and caverns located within the hollow interior of our planet. To do this, we must locate its entrance, situated somewhere around the North Pole. Once inside, Thompson explains, there's a labyrinth of caverns and caves illuminated by glowing moss.

Our Inner Earth operates on a completely different time frame, he says. Inner Earth tribes typically live for between 800 to 1,600 years, as they're protected from cosmic

112

Dallas Thompson planned to journey into the centre of the Earth using a modified SoloTrek personal helicopter. Once inside the mantle, he wouldn't need fuel as the 'copter would be powered by electromagnetic energy and navigated by Inner Earth beings.

rays. Woolly mammoths roam free, and pterodactyls stalk the skies. 'How do you know all of this?' Bell asks. 'I know because I know because I know,' replies Thompson.

Thompson is so convinced of the existence of this Inner Earth that he's planning to travel there, despite also claiming to be 'legally blind', his retinas having been burned by an intense light at the time of his car accident. On 24 May 2003, he says, he will set out towards the Arctic on a mission to discover the 'hole in the pole' – an entrance that is both an actual 'real hole' and a 'dimensional portal that merges into a higher vibration and frequency'.

To journey inside, he's going to use a modified SoloTrek personal helicopter, a first-of-its-kind jetpack he's already acquired thanks to private investment. Once inside the mantle, his backpack 'copter won't even need fuel, as it will be powered by electromagnetic energy and navigated by the Inner Earth beings. The only problem he might face, he says, is that the hole is guarded by 'inter-dimensional security', taking the form of mechanical swarming bees, and they know that he's coming.

Over the next hour Thompson's monologues become ever more manic and unsettling. He even begins to refer to himself in the plural: 'We've been really busy here,' he says, repeatedly plugging his book, *The Cosmic Manuscript*, which he claims is flying off the shelves. He also starts to pepper his speech with hyperbolical statements: 'I'm pretty much well known all over the world now,' he tells Bell. 'I don't sleep, I just meditate.' It's becoming increasingly clear that Dallas Thompson is the type of guy you really wouldn't want to get stuck in a conversation with on a night bus.

Soon after the radio interview, the media become interested in Thompson and his planned expedition. *The Cosmic Manuscript* apparently sells by the thousands. Two months later, our excitable radio guest reports to his Yahoo Group that he's getting over 5,000 emails per day and, in an unexpected twist, announces that he's decided to pull his supposed bestseller from sale. Shortly afterwards, Dallas Thompson disappears and is never heard from again.

BELIEF THAT THE Earth is hollow and populated by strange and brilliant beings has been bubbling away for centuries. It's possible that the origins of such beliefs lie in shamanic traditions in which medicine men or women would recount to the community their heroic journeys into a mysterious netherworld. Here they would encounter both benign and hostile spirits, undergo death and rebirth, and finally return endowed with great powers. Certainly, the idea of a hollow underworld has inspired some of our best-known science fiction, including Jules Verne's *Journey to*

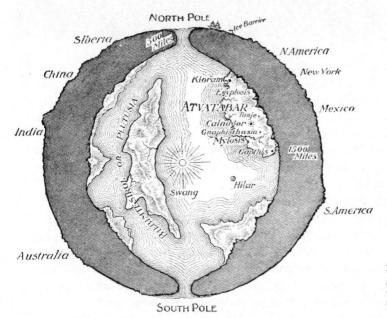

A map of 'The Interior World', from *The Goddess of Atvatabar*, a science-fiction novel by William Bradshaw (1892).

Astronomer Edmund Halley was the first to propose that the Earth was made up of spherical layers, each with its own atmosphere and capable of supporting life.

the Centre of the Earth (1864), Edgar Rice Burroughs's *At the Earth's Core* (1914) and Edgar Allan Poe's *The Narrative of Arthur Gordon Pym of Nantucket* (1838). Common themes describe a land of endless subterranean caverns and tunnels, replete with woolly mammoths and pterodactyls, and crystal cities populated by lost races of humans. Curiously, the scientific hypothesis of a hollow Earth kept respectability up until the early 1800s, and many of the fantasy stories actually drew on these real theories as jumping-off points.

In 1692 English scientist Edmund Halley (of comet fame) became the first to propose that the Earth was not only hollow but made up of spherical layers. Noticing the unpredictability of the Earth's magnetic fields, he decided to blame this on the nature of our hollow planet. Halley argued that the Earth comprised of an outer shell (where we live) with three further inner crusts inside, each with its own atmosphere and capable of supporting life – a little like a Russian doll or a Kinder Egg. It was the poles of these three 'inner Earths' that kept throwing out his experiments.

Later, another thinker proposed that we are already inside the Earth. Cyrus Reed

Teed was an American electric physician and alchemist whose unconventional experiments often involved dangerous levels of electricity. In 1869 he electrocuted himself so badly that he blacked out. When he regained consciousness, he claimed to have had a divine illumination. God, taking on the form of comely women, had urged him to use his scientific knowledge to pioneer a new understanding of our universe.

He went on to launch his Cellular Cosmogony theory, a belief that human beings were actually living inside a giant hollow sphere rather than on the planet's surface. He proposed that we were held in place by centrifugal force rather than gravity, and that our world was heated by a giant battery-operated sun.

John Cleves Symmes 1780–1829

While it's unlikely that Dallas Thompson ever set out on his expedition, other Hollow Earth pioneers have ventured further – some claiming to have flown over the entrances, while others have mounted expeditions to descend into the centre of our planet without so much as a canary for safety.

One of the earliest aspiring Inner Earth explorers was US Army captain John Cleves Symmes. A war veteran and unsuccessful trader, in 1818 Symmes issued a pamphlet titled 'Circular Number 1', sending copies to notable governments, royalty, colleges and philosophical societies around the world. He opened his letter boldly, addressing it 'TO ALL THE WORLD!', and then went on to say:

LIGHT GIVES LIGHT, TO LIGHT DISCOVER—" AD INFINITUM."

ST. LOUIS, (Missouri Territory,)
North America, April 10, A. D. 1818.

TO ALL THE WORLD!
I declare the earth is hollow, and habitable within ; containing a number of solid concentrick spheres, one within the other, and that it is open at the poles 12 or 16 degrees ; I pledge my life in support of this truth, and am ready to explore the hollow, if the world will support and aid me in the undertaking.

Jno. Cleves Symmes

Of Ohio, late Captain of Infantry.

N. B.—I have ready for the press, a Treatise on the principles of matter, wherein I show proofs of the above positions, account for various phenomena, and disclose *Doctor Darwin's Golden Secret.*

My terms, are the patronage of this and the new worlds.

I dedicate to my Wife and her ten Children.

I select *Doctor S. L. Mitchell, Sir H. Davy* and *Baron Alex. de Humboldt*, as my protectors.

I ask one hundred brave companions, well equipped, to start from Siberia in the fall season, with Reindeer and slays, on the ice of the frozen sea ; I engage we find warm and rich land, stocked with thrifty vegetables and animals if not men, on reaching one degree northward of latitude 82 ; we will return in the succeeding spring.

J. C. S.

John Cleves Symmes sent his bold letter 'to all the world': posting copies to notable governments, royal rulers, colleges and philosophical societies.

116

One unexpected result of Symmes's Hollow Earth conviction was that it inadvertently led to the launch of the 'United States Exploring Expedition', which in turn led to the establishment of the Smithsonian Institute.

I declare that the earth is hollow and habitable within; containing a number of solid concentric spheres, one within the other, and that it is open at the poles 12 or 16 degrees. I pledge my life in support of this truth, and am ready to explore the hollow, if the world will support and aid me in the undertaking.
Circular Number 1

Symmes claimed that there were openings at the poles through which one could access these inner lands, which became known as 'Symmes Holes'. Launching a campaign to garner support – which comprised of publishing further pamphlets, giving lectures and touring with a handmade wooden globe that came apart to reveals its hidden layers – Symmes proposed that he should lead an expedition to the North Pole to prove his theory, during which he hoped to discover one of these openings and enter the Inner Earth:

I ask 100 brave companions to start from Siberia … with reindeers and sleighs, on the ice of the frozen sea; I engage we find a warm, rich land, stocked with thrifty vegetables and animals, if not men, on reaching one degree north of latitude 82.
Quoted in 'Going Underground', The Guardian, *16 June 2005*

Symmes's followers began to petition government to finance his expedition and they got as far as having Congress vote on whether to release funds in 1822. Unfortunately,

Rear Admiral Richard Byrd (*right*), on an expedition to the Antarctic, Austral summer 1946–7.

Symmes's plea was turned down, though he continued to campaign until his death in 1849. One unexpected result of his conviction, however, was that it inadvertently led to the launch of the 'United States Exploring Expedition' – commissioned to explore the South Pacific – which in turn led to the establishment of a national museum of natural history, the Smithsonian Institute.

Admiral Richard Byrd 1888–1957

Over three hundred years after Halley first touted the idea, there's still a bevy of Hollow Earthers valiantly fighting their corner on websites and forums. There are common themes in the world they describe, usually boiling down to a tropical paradise inhabited by peaceful and hyper-intelligent beings. Some describe a race of arboreal people – willowy chaps with branches for hands; others talk of tall, amiable humans with unbelievably long lifespans. A handful even claim that the Nazis escaped inside the Earth, and Hitler is currently kicking back with the woolly mammoths.

Many believers evidence a secret journal written in 1947 by Admiral Richard Byrd, who claimed to be the first person not only to fly over the North and South Poles, but also (according to the hushed-up diary entries) to pass over one of the Symmes Holes.

Byrd was a well-respected explorer, a US naval officer and navigation expert. In 1926 Byrd completed the first ever, albeit contested, flight over the North Pole. Then, in 1929, he became the first pilot to fly to the South Pole and back again. He was trailblazing and brave, and was considered reliable by those who knew him; he was even decorated with the Medal of Honour, the highest decoration bestowed by the USA.

According to Hollow Earthers, in February 1947 Byrd also traversed one of the Symmes Holes, being guided by an intelligence within, where he observed lush lakes, enormous trees and herds of woolly mammoths. Supposedly, in a journal that was quickly snaffled away by the government, Byrd writes that the Earth is like a bead with holes at each end and that you can travel right through it like a needle and thread. The Northern Lights are reflections of the thriving cities inside our planet.

Official reports place Byrd at the South Pole at the time when the diary was supposedly written, where he was establishing an Antarctic research base, so it sounds unlikely. However, in a later interview, Byrd claims to have discovered a completely unexplored area of land the size of America beyond the South Pole. 'There's a lot of adventure left, down at the bottom of the world,' he says. 'An untouched reservoir of natural resources.'

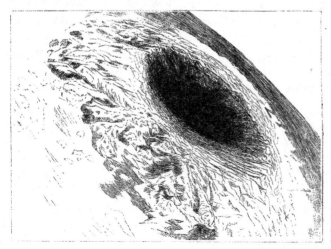

'Symme's Hole, as it would appear to a Lunarian with a telescope' (*Harper's New Monthly Magazine*, 1882).

Rodney M. Cluff

One particularly interesting follower of Admiral Byrd's observations is New Mexico resident Rodney M. Cluff, who has attempted two expeditions to the centre of the Earth. Cluff found evidence of the real nature of our Earth within scriptures. Among those living inside, he says, are Germans – refugees from the Second World War – as well as Viking colonists from Greenland. 'Obviously, there has to be some Inuit down there, because whenever they were asked where they came from they would point north and say, they were from the land where the sun never goes down,' he told *Vice*.

The opening lines on his website named 'World Top Secret Our Earth IS Hollow!' reads:

Located at 84.84 degrees North and South Latitude are Polar Openings that lead into the hollow interior of our planet where the Lost Ten Tribes of Israel today dwell in perfect harmony, with life spans equal to those of the Methuselahs of the Bible, whose only desire is to live in peace. Their flying saucers in defense of their country at times are seen on our surface world. They don't come to destroy, they are waiting…

ourhollowearth.com

Believing there to be 'substantial openings' at both the North and South poles, Cluff set off in 1981, together with his wife and five children, and headed to Alaska. Once there, he met with others who had travelled with the same intention. Speaking with Will Storr from *The Telegraph* in 2014 he recounts the beginning of their journey: 'We started on the road up to Point Barrow,' he told Will Storr in a phone interview. 'We saw a sign, at one point, saying "This Is a Private Road: Don't Go Any Further." So we didn't go any further.' How long did he drive before he reached the sign and aborted the mission? asks the now-incredulous journalist. 'About an hour,' Cluff replies, to a resounding silence.

His second attempt, over 20 years later, was rather more ambitious, and perhaps a little more thoroughly planned. The seed was sown following an email conversation in 2003, with explorer Steve Currey who had inherited his family's travel company. Over the next few years, the pair planned their 'Voyage to the Hollow Earth', and began recruiting members.

The trip was all set to embark in 2007 and started selling places for $26,000 a pop. Astonishingly, around 40 people signed up. Although, to be fair, it was a pretty tempting itinerary. Members of the expedition would go in search of the 'most plausible location for a north polar opening that leads into the interior of the earth', which would be located at 84.4 N Latitude, 141 E Longitude. The location is based on a supposedly 'true account' of the Norwegian fisherman Olaf Jansen's encounters with giants living inside our Earth, in Willis George Emmerson's *The Smoky God* (1908). While many recognize the book to be a work of fiction, the Hollow Earthers take it as fact ('Going Underground').

The 24-day trip, starting 26 June 2007, had time for sightseeing in Moscow, followed by a voyage on a Russian icebreaker that cut 'through ice like butter' and three days allocated to searching for the hole. Once there, they would conduct scientific observations in order to 'resolve once and for all whether the Hollow Earth theory has any validity'. After the hole was located, days 12 to 18 were allocated to travelling up the Hiddekel river to the City of Jehu, and taking 'a monorail trip to City of Eden to visit the Palace of the King of the Inner World'.

There was the back-up plan, of course, should they fail to locate the opening: 'Please note that if we are unable to find the Polar opening,' it states in the itinerary, 'we will be returning via the New Siberian Islands to visit skeleton remains of exotic animals thought to originate from Inner Earth.'

Tragically, expedition leader Steve Currey discovered that he had six inoperable brain tumours and passed away before he and Cluff could embark on their initial recce to locate the opening. The trip then suffered two further setbacks: a key fundraiser, Dr Brooks Agnew, pulled his support after his own stockholders heard rumours of his being involved; another team member died in a plane crash. Cluff

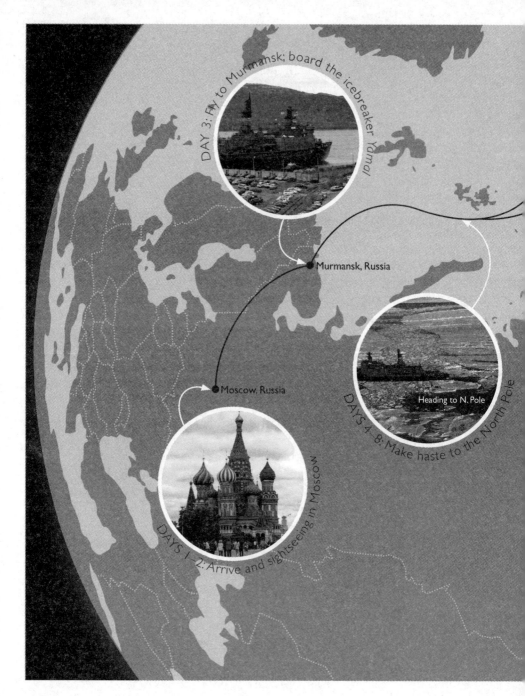

DAY 3: Fly to Murmansk; board the icebreaker *Yamal*

Murmansk, Russia

Heading to N. Pole

DAYS 4–8: Make haste to the North Pole

Moscow, Russia

DAYS 1–2: Arrive and sightseeing in Moscow

NORTH POLAR OPENING
AT 84.4 N LAT. 141 E LONG.

DAYS 9–18: Search for the North Polar
Opening – the adventure begins!*

New Siberian Islands

*Or return via the New Siberian Islands to visit Inner Earth skeletons if unable to find the polar opening

VOYAGE TO HOLLOW EARTH EXPEDITION

The trip, set to launch in 2007, promised
the opportunity to take a monorail trip to
the capital of our Inner World, plus sightseeing
time in Moscow.

was convinced something mysterious was happening. 'There seems to be some force that's trying to stop this happening,' he told *The Telegraph*. 'I think it's the international bankers. They don't want the Inner Earth people messing around with their slaves, here on the outer world.'

Despite these knockbacks, Cluff hasn't given up, remaining hopeful that one day he will secure funding as well as a new expedition leader who can help him get past the 'no entry' signs to Hollow Earth.

BUT WHAT ABOUT the fate of Dallas Thompson, our plucky Inner Earth fanatic? After he disappeared, fellow Hollow Earthers began to speculate on online forums about whether the personal trainer had put himself in danger, having unearthed too much truth, or whether he had, in fact, completed his mission and was presently frolicking with woolly mammoths beneath the mantle. The answer for his sudden retreat may prove be much more mundane, however; with key clues to be found rather unexpectedly on the bookselling website Amazon.

While it remained on sale, Thompson's book, *The Cosmic Manuscript*, garnered a wealth of gushing reviews: 'I am a Doctor who has read thousads [*sic*] of books, and Cosmic Mauscript [*sic*] is in a class of its own because its Author [*sic*] is legally blind, and so confident that you would never know [*sic*]' writes 'John', an educated man who, despite reading 'thousads' of books, has only found time to write one Amazon review. In fact, astonishingly, not one of the reviewers – who include a Native American elder and a listener who happened to tune into *Coast to Coast AM* and has since 'read [the book] over three times, and I will read it another five times' – have commented on any other titles on Amazon, having seemingly created profiles especially to share their thoughts on *The Cosmic Manuscript*.

One can't help but draw comparisons between the tone of the reviews and Thompson's own breathless monologues on *Coast to Coast*. Every one of the comments includes phrases that mirror the author's way of speaking. 'I wish for him Love, Light, Peace and Compassion on his journey,' says 'CarolB', while 'Dina' writes 'Greetings from the garden of lilies and purple butterflies! ... You have held me safe and warm under your wing, feeding me with the water of love, light and hope.'

However, among the glowing, five-star appraisals there simmers an accusation – that Thompson has plagiarized the content of his book. In one deleted review, 'W M Mott' writes: 'Material in this "book" was plagiarized, lifted, STOLEN, word-for-word, from previously published materials. The "author" is IN HIDING as a result, and refuses to surface for fear of well-deserved lawsuits' (quoted in 'Hollow Earth Conspiracy Theories: The Hole Trust', *The Telegraph*, 13 July 2014).

Mott continues to accuse Thompson of lifting entire pages and paragraphs from his own earlier book, *Caverns, Cauldrons and Concealed Creatures: A Study of Subterranean*

Mysteries in History, Folklore and Myth. Could Dallas Thompson be in hiding, fearing a costly court case? Or is he, in fact, flying free around our Inner Earth in his fuel-less helicopter backpack and keeping company with people who have branches for arms? As Thompson would be expected to live another 1,500 or so years, it might take a little while for the truth to come to the surface. *JT*

SEEKER'S DIRECTORY

Books
Journey to the Centre of the Earth, Jules Verne (Pierre-Jules Hetzel, 1864)
German professor Otto Lidenbrock believes there to be volcanic tubes going toward the centre of the Earth and decides to descend into the Icelandic volcano Snæfellsjökull in order to locate them. A genre of subterranean fiction existed well before the book's release, but it's fair to say that Verne's popular novel considerably added to its popularity and influenced later writings.

At the Earth's Core, Edgar Rice Burroughs (A. C. McClurg, 1914)
A pulp fantasy epic, and the first in Burroughs's series about the fictional 'Hollow Earth' land of Pellucidar – a world of prehistoric creatures, ape-like Sagoths and Amazonian women.

Radio
Dallas Thompson talks to Art Bell on *Coast to Coast AM* (4 October 2002)
Well worth a listen: https://soundcloud.com/bob-da-builda/dallas-thompson-art-bell-into

Public Domain
The online journal and not-for-profit project, *The Public Domain Review,* has oodles of archive resources for the curious including essays by Peter Fitting, author of *Subterranean Worlds: A Critical Anthology,* and Brook Wilensky-Lanford, author of *Paradise Lust: Searching for the Garden of Eden,* plus links to original texts. **publicdomainreview.org**

Journeys of love and loss

*Marina Abramović and Ulay: the lovers who walked
1,550 miles in order to split up*

During the mid-1970s, a Portuguese fisherman learned of the murder of his son, who had been holidaying in America; a bungled mugging had led to tragedy. Seeking some kind of resolution, he flew to Buffalo, on the shores of Lake Erie, to visit the location of his son's death. Along with his grief, he felt a gnawing regret that the pair hadn't been closer; political differences had kept them apart for many years. As he lingered in Buffalo, mourning, days became weeks. Finally, he decided to buy a camper van and, without really planning it, began journeying around the Great Lakes. Every day he would talk to people he met, walk, swim, fish and process his emotions. It would be six years before he returned to his old life. 'I needed to find some kind of meaning out there. What the point of a life really was,' he told a close friend. 'It finally came to me. In two words: be kind.'

P. K. Mahanandia and Charlotte von Schedvin

Around the same time in India, Delhi street artist P. K. Mahanandia was drawing a Swedish tourist, Charlotte von Schedvin, when he decided to ask her about her life. Having been told by his clairvoyant mother that his one great love would be a musical Taurian who owned a jungle and came from a faraway land, Mahanandia discovered Schedvin to be a piano-playing Swede whose family owned a forest. And yes, her star sign was Taurus. Mahanandia insisted on inviting her round for tea, and within a week the pair had fallen in love. When Schedvin finally had to return home to Sweden, Mahanandia promised to join her there. Without sufficient funds for a plane flight however, he was stuck in India.

Schedvin offered to pay for his airfare but Mahanandia would have none of it; he was too proud to accept. Three agonizing years passed until, finally, Mahanandia was able to sell all of his worldly possessions in exchange for a second-hand

Delhi street artist P. K. Mahanandia, who undertook a 7,000-mile (11,625-km) bike ride through the Middle East and Europe in order to be reunited with his true love, Charlotte von Schedvin.

bicycle. He went on to undertake a 7,000-mile (11,625-km) journey, cycling through the Middle East and Europe, while scraping together enough money for food by selling his street art. Six months later, the lovers were reunited and married. Now in their sixties, the pair claim to be as much in love today as when they first met in India 40 years ago.

When asked why he wanted to climb Everest, following a reconnaissance expedition and a first failed attempt, mountaineer George Mallory famously replied: 'Because it's there.' But while the simple reward of adventure, as well as the inevitable fame and fortune, may continue to motivate many an intrepid journey, what of love – and of loss? The power of devotion, and grief, has inspired countless courageous and singular journeys over the years. When someone is gripped by love or loss, as we're about to see, no journey seems too great.

Marina Abramović and Ulay

From the moment that the respectively Serbian and West German performance artists Marina Abramović and Ulay (Frank Uwe Laysiepen) clapped eyes on each other, in Amsterdam in 1975, they were inseparable. Ulay found Abramović witchy and otherworldly; she found him wild and exciting. Even their initial encounter was propitious; they met on their shared birthday: 30 November.

Marina Abramović and Ulay collaborated in performances that put them in precarious and physically demanding situations, to see how they and the audience would respond. In one, called '*Relation in Time*', they remained tied together by their hair for 17 hours.

Inevitably, the pair began to perform together, describing themselves as a 'two-headed body', sometimes dressing and acting as if they were twins. For four years they lived a nomadic lifestyle, travelling across Europe in a corrugated-iron van and performing in villages and towns.

Their artistic collaborations matched their personalities – they focused on performances that put them in precarious and physically demanding situations, to see how they and the audience would respond. In one, called '*Relation in Time*', they remained tied together by their hair for 17 hours. In another, they blocked their nostrils with cigarette filters and embraced in a carbon-dioxide fuelled kiss for 20 minutes, before coming close to passing out. They also explored conflict, again taking their ideas to extremes: they screamed at one another in front of audiences until their voices were hoarse; they ran full pelt into each other, naked; they slapped each other's faces until they could take no more. One time, Ulay held a bow and arrow, primed at Abramović's heart; one slip and he could have killed her. Deeply uncomfortable viewing, this was relationship therapy played out as art – and, perhaps, vice versa.

IN 1983 Abramović and Ulay announced their ultimate collaboration: *The Lovers*. They proposed to be the first people to walk the Great Wall of China. Setting off alone from opposite ends, they planned to meet in the middle where they would marry. Exhilarated by the emotional and physical scale of *The Lovers*, the pair imagined themselves walking alone across great expanses of the Chinese landscape, camping under the stars and concluding the journey with the ultimate commitment. They saw *The Lovers* as an odyssey and a performance in which they alone would be the players and audience. For Abramović it would be, 'the apotheosis of romantic love' (Thomas McEvilley's essay in *The Lovers*, exhibition catalogue, 1989).

Eager to prepare, and ever practical, Ulay shipped a year's supply of dried tofu and seaweed to China, together with tents and camping stoves. What the pair were less prepared for, however, was Chinese bureaucracy.

At the time, China was a closed shop to the West, and the authorities in Beijing struggled to comprehend the pair's motives for the journey. No one camped, or walked, the Great Wall as an 'art project'. And who in their right minds would want to get married on it? Paper trails were endless. Permissions and visas were granted then denied. As phone calls, letters and documents were fired back and forth between the Chinese authorities and the two artists, time rolled on.

The following year, Abramović and Ulay discovered that a Chinese railway clerk had quashed their desire to be the first to walk the wall in its entirety by completing the trek himself. Ulay quietly accused the Chinese man of plagiarism. The country's bureaucrats were, by now, forcing the pair to make some serious compromises to their plans. The artists were told in no uncertain terms that it would be too dangerous to do the walk alone and they would be required to have an accompanying crew. Sections of the wall close to military bases would also be out of bounds. In these instances, they would be collected by jeep and taken to the next section of the wall to continue their walk.

In 1986 the pair ventured out to China to visit parts of the Great Wall, to familiarize themselves with it and to meet some of the villagers they would be staying with. Permission was finally granted for the walk to take place the following year, before, inexplicably, authorities postponed it again. A frustrated Ulay confessed, 'I have been living on the wall in my thoughts for five years. Already I feel I have walked it ten times. Already it is worn, it is polished' (*On Edge: Performance at the Edge of the 20th Century*, C. Carr, Wesleyan University Press, 1989).

Finally, having also agreed to participate in a film of their 'study' of the Great Wall for Chinese Central Television, they were granted permission.

ABRAMOVIĆ AND ULAY began their walks on 30 March 1988, from either ends of the Great Wall, better known to the Chinese as the Sleeping Dragon. Abramović, at the dragon's head, set off westwards from the Yellow Sea. Dressed in baggy red clothes, she was soon given the nickname 'Pa Ma Ta Je' – big fat sister mother – by her entourage.

Much of her trek proved arduous. Abramović was walking through the mountainous regions of western China. Denied the opportunity to camp, she was accommodated in villages and hostels each night, which often required a two-hour trek just to get back to the wall. On such difficult and inaccessible terrain, she had to watch every step. Slipping over rocks like polished ice on her fourth day, Abramović and her guide found themselves hanging by their fingertips over an abyss.

Abramović found homes and stables built into sections of the winding wall. Other parts had been dismantled by locals who, under Mao's encouragement to 'kill the dragon', had removed the clay and stones for building. Once, Abramović claimed to have walked through a kilometre of human bones.

At every village she stayed in, Abramović requested to meet its oldest resident and asked them to share a local legend. Inevitably these were dragon stories, often related to the wall itself. While built as a defence to keep out the Mongol hordes, the serpentine spine of the Great Wall had been carefully mapped out by geomancers for its 'dragon energy'. Abramović would occasionally find copper pots placed along the wall, planted there as energy spots – acupuncture points to control the energy that rippled up and down the creature's back.

Some 3,100 miles (5,000 km) west of Abramović, Ulay had started his walk at the dragon's tail. Most of his journey would be spent trekking through China's deserts. Rickshaws and donkeys were familiar sights, as were camels pulling ploughs. Ulay crossed the great Yellow River on a raft covered with sheepskins, and, like Abramović, saw families living in caves within the wall itself. He managed to sleep under the stars some nights, while his bemused crew watched over him from their jeeps. Most of the time, however, Ulay was forced to sleep in nearby villages. Fragmented by bureaucracy and restrictions, the walk was not the romantic sojourn the pair had dreamed of, though they had little choice but to play along.

Of the two, Ulay found it more frustrating. At the top of his staff, he placed a white flag, there as a reminder to surrender to the guides and keep his anger in check. Once, when physically restrained from climbing a mountain range, which he'd been told was unsafe, Ulay lost his temper and snapped his staff in rage. His anger and sense of isolation was rooted in more than just 'artistic temperament'. Moustachioed and lean, with long hair and bright blue matching drawstring trousers and cape, to a Westerner Ulay would have looked every part the bohemian traveller. To the Chinese, however, Ulay and Abramović were alien travellers from another planet. On occasions, Ulay was made to eat separately from his host family because the authorities feared the risk of 'contamination' from his Western ways, or so he believed. Ulay complained:

Am I like some strange animal to them? Every encounter I have with innocent people here, the stranger I become. This inability of making friends remains unsolved.
The Great Wall: Lovers at the Brink *(dir. Murray Grigor, 1990)*

Ulay and Abramović were, however, objects of great curiosity to all who encountered them. Having originally believed themselves to be the sole players and audience for their walk, everything the pair did was witnessed as if a performance. In towns and villages, silent crowds followed them wherever they went. In one settlement, villagers gathered to watch Abramović sleep. When she awoke, a different group were present, silently staring at her.

Despite the many niggles, peasant life evoked in Ulay a growing desire for a quiet, rural existence in his own life. The simplicity of the trek had stirred his soul. Abramović, on the other hand, enjoyed staying with the peasant families but came to hate China's 'ugliness'. It was, for her, depressingly similar to the bleakness and sobriety of the Soviet-run Yugoslavia where she had grown up. And yet, despite the endless days of silence and walking, neither claimed to have spent much time thinking about each other.

More by happenstance than planning, Ulay and Abramović met at the centre of a stone bridge in Shenmu in Shaanxi Province, nestled among a series of temples built in the Ming Dynasty. They had averaged 12½ miles (20 km) per day, walked 90 days and covered roughly 1,550 miles (2,500 km) each. As they embraced affectionately,

In 1983 Abramović and Ulay announced their ultimate collaboration: *The Lovers*. They proposed to be the first people to walk the Great Wall, meeting in the middle, where they would marry.

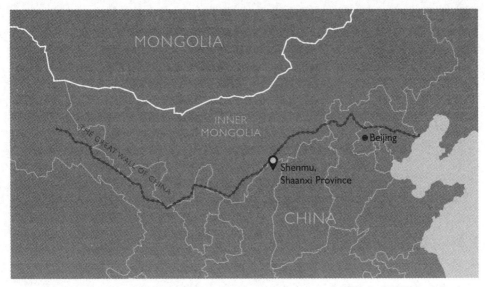

Ulay and Abramović averaged 12½ miles (20 km) per day, walked 90 days and covered roughly 1,550 miles (2,500 km) each. Despite the endless days of silence and walking, neither claimed to have spent much time thinking about the other.

Ulay shared with Abramović his desire to continue his walk for ever. Abramović was unequivocal in her desire to leave China as soon as was humanly possible. Ulay made a comment about her shoes that seemed to annoy her; to his irritation, she began to cry.

While musicians, the Chinese press and even a fireworks display had been laid on for the pair, there would to be no wedding ceremony. After a press conference in Beijing, they returned separately to Amsterdam and didn't speak or see one another for 22 years. What had gone wrong?

IN THE FIVE years that Ulay and Abramović had been waiting for permission for the walk, their lives had changed irrevocably. Their work had become internationally renowned and Abramović welcomed the success. While she was fed up with being the archetypical poor artist, Ulay had no interest in celebrity. An anarchist who enjoyed solitude, he rebelled against what he saw as a growing commercialization of their work. In short, they had grown apart. Both had had affairs; communication and trust broke down.

However, Ulay and Abramović were not the kind of couple to willingly admit defeat. They decided to go ahead with the walk not in order to marry but to spilt up. *The Lovers* transformed from wedding to a divorce. 'Why didn't you just make a phone call and break up like normal people,' one friend had allegedly quipped. That simply wasn't their style.

To the Chinese, the dragon is an auspicious symbol, representing power, good fortune and the elemental forces of nature. Walking the dragon's spine had, for Ulay and Abramović, been intended as a great motif for transcending the barriers that divide us – it was to be a totem of love and reconnection. Instead, the wall came to represent a division in myriad forms, not just physical but also the cultural and political barriers between East and West, as well as the emotional barriers that had grown between the pair. Since planning to walk the wall, the artists' differences had become more apparent and more difficult to reconcile. Ulay was practical; Abramović chaotic. The latter embraced the growing success of their work; the former withdrew from it.

In Western mythology the dragon is perceived differently. It is a symbol of malevolence and impotence – a destructive, jealous creature to be hunted down and killed. Abramović claimed that the idea for *The Lovers* came to her in a dream, a vision in which the pair would wake a sleeping dragon through their epic walk. They had, it seems, woken the wrong dragon.

Over the next two decades Abramović's work continued to reach larger and larger audiences; her celebrity grew. She becomes a mentor to Lady Gaga and Jay-Z, made adverts for Adidas and came to be known as 'the grandmother of performance art'.

In 2010, at a MOMA retrospective of her work, entitled '*The Artist Is Present*', Abramović sat for eight hours a day – nearly 740 hours in total – in silence, in a table at the museum. Members of the public were invited to come and sit at the opposite end and hold her gaze. The show was spiritual and cathartic for some; pretentious and self-indulgent to others. Many queued for hours for the opportunity to sit opposite Abramović for a few minutes or, in a few cases – and to the irritation of those in the queue – the whole day.

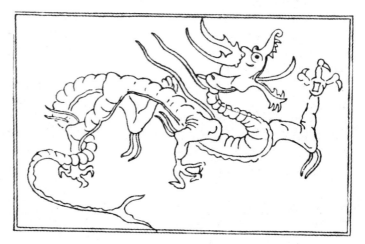

Walking the dragon's spine (the Great Wall) had, for Ulay and Abramović, been intended as a totem of love and reconnection.

In *The Artist Is Present*, Abramović sat silent and still for 736 hours and 30 minutes, while spectators were invited to take turns sitting opposite her.

There were plenty of tears. One man visited 21 times and had the tally tattooed on his arm. One moment, however, was to totally capture audiences' attention, gaining hundreds of thousands of views when it was posted online. On the opening night of the show, Ulay unexpectedly stepped from the audience to sit and face his former lover. He nervously stretched his legs, adjusted his jacket and, as Abramović opened her eyes to see him, the pair smiled. It was the first time in 22 years that they had seen each other. Tears filled their eyes.

Finally, Abramović, in a flowing blood-red dress, broke her own rules by leaning across and taking Ulay's hands. Onlookers broke into applause. It is impossible to watch the video of this moment without also being drawn to tears. After a 3,100-mile (5,000 km) journey in order to break up, the pair had been reunited by just a few small steps. Over the years that followed friendship and intimacy was rekindled. A new dragon had been awakened. *DB*

Book

The Lovers, Thomas McEvilley, Marina Abramović and Ulay (Stedelijk Van Abbemuseum Publishers, 1983)

Art

Marina Abramović: The Artist Is Present (2010)
A performance piece in which Abramović sat silent and still for 736 hours and 30 minutes, while spectators were invited to take turns sitting opposite her. Ulay made a surprise appearance at the opening night of the show. It's available to watch on YouTube, and if you can watch this moment without crying you probably have the necessary qualifications for being a traffic warden.

The final fix

William Burroughs and Allen Ginsberg: the Amazon-bound psychonauts who sampled 'God's flesh' | Richard Evans Schultes: the fearless ethnobotanist who sought out the 'vine of the soul' | Gordon Wasson: the mushroom obsessive who catalysed a psychedelic revolution

Dear Allen, I stopped off to have my piles out. Wouldn't do to go back amongst the Indians with piles I figured.'
William Burroughs, 15 January 1953, Hotel Colon, Panama, in The Yage Letters, *1963*

William Burroughs 1914–1997

In the winter of 1953 Beat author and junkie William Burroughs undertook a six-month journey through South America in search of a sacred plant: yage, or ayahuasca as it is better known. Burroughs had been inspired by a paper written by a then unknown Harvard graduate to head deep into unchartered (for westerners) territories of the Amazon in search of ayahuasca.

The plant had been an integral part of indigenous rituals and customs for thousands of years and was alleged to have mind-expanding and healing properties, the power to slow down time and even to give the user telepathic powers.'Yage may be the final fix,' Burroughs wrote, at the end of his first novel, *Junkie*. Not only was he hoping that ayahuasca would help him kick his opium addiction, Burroughs also understood it to be a great visionary tool. And he had no intention of 'seeing eternity in a grain of sand' with his piles playing up.

The journey didn't go quite according to plan. Burroughs rattled around Panama, Peru and Columbia, drifting from bar to bar, contracting malaria and neuritis, spending four days in hospital 'junk sick' in Bogotá, getting 'rolled for money' by rent boys, beaten up, and even jailed for two days for having lost his documents. When he was finally able to pack his snake bite serum, penicillin, hammock, tula (napsack) and head into the Columbian jungle, Burroughs was 'conned by medicine men'.

Beat author, visual artist and junkie William Burroughs, who in the winter of 1953 undertook a six-month journey through South America in search of a sacred plant: yage, or ayahuasca as it is better known.

Allen Ginsberg 1926–1997

He wrote wearily of these experiences in letters to his friend, the poet Allen Ginsberg, bemoaning 'this nation of kleptomaniacs'. While Burroughs's tone was typically sardonic, in South America it was heightened from the death of his

The preparation of ayahuasca. When Burroughs drank the mixture, he wrote of 'vividness of mental imagery, aphrodisiac results, silliness and giggling' (*The Yage Letters*).

wife less than a year previously, when he had accidentally shot and killed her in a drunken game of William Tell. Another reason for the journey into South America was to deal with the guilt.

Burroughs's fortune finally changed in Bogota when, by good fortune, he met the young Harvard ethnobotanist who had inspired him to go there. Together they embarked on a 1,000-mile (1,600-km) expedition in search of ayahuasca, although when Burroughs finally got to sample the plant's mind-altering powers, the experience was far from pleasant:

> It was like going under ether ... I was hit by violent, sudden nausea and rushed for the door ... I felt numb as if I was covered with layers of cotton ... Larval beings passed before my eyes in a blue haze, each one giving an obscene, mocking squawk ... I must have vomited six times.
> *Burroughs and Ginsberg,* The Yage Letters

Undeterred, the next night he drank again (though only a third of the previous night's dosage) and experienced, 'vividness of mental imagery, aphrodisiac results, silliness and giggling' (*The Yage Letters*).

By July, he had arrived in Lima and drank the last of his mixture. This time Burroughs

To prepare ayahuasca, sections of *Banisteriopsis caapi* vine are macerated and boiled alone or with leaves from any of a number of other plants, to create a brew that contains the powerful psychedelic drug DMT.

came close to the ecstatic visions he had read about. In another letter to Allen Ginsberg he wrote:

> Yage (ayuhuasca) is space time travel. The blood and substance of many races … new races as yet unconceived and unborn. Migrations, incredible journeys through deserts and jungles and mountains … across the Pacific in an outrigger canoe to Easter Island.
> *Burroughs and Ginsberg*, The Yage Letters

When Ginsberg followed in Burroughs footsteps seven years later he too was overwhelmed by what he described as a 'schizophrenic alteration of consciousness'. 'I began seeing or feeling what I thought was the great being … I wish I knew who, if anyone knows, who I am or what I am' (*The Yage Letters*).

Shaken by the plant's effects Ginsberg wrote to Burroughs asking for his advice on how to process the experience. Burroughs reminded him of the last words of the 12th-century Islamic prophet Hassan Sabbah: 'Nothing is true, everything is permitted.' Whether this helped or not isn't documented, although, years later, reflecting back on their experiences with ayahuasca in the Amazon, both men claimed to have had a transformative shift of consciousness. In an open letter penned in 1963, Ginsberg wrote: 'The ayahuasca trance state of 1960 was prophetic of transfiguration of self-consciousness from homeless mind sensation of eternal fright to incarnate body feeling present bliss now actualized.'

Within a few decades, mass pilgrimages to the Amazon in search of the transformative effects of ayahuasca and other psychotropic plants would become a rite of passage for a new generation of psychonauts. After centuries of hostility from white settlers and the suppression of traditional customs and rituals by missionaries, some of the indigenous people of the Amazon region would be sought out anew, for their knowledge, teachings and psychedelic brews. But to explain how we got there, first we need to travel back a little further in time.

Richard Evans Schultes 1915–2001

The ethnobotanist who had inspired Burroughs and Ginsberg to undertake such perilous journeys of both mind and body was Richard Evans Schultes. Often dubbed the godfather of ethnobotany – the study of indigenous people and their use of plants – Schultes was a fearless explorer who spent the best part of 20 years travelling through some of the remotest regions of South America and Mexico in search of elusive and semi-mythical hallucinogenic plants and fungi. Schultes participated in countless sacred ceremonies with indigenous groups, and was one of the first Westerners to treat both the people and their rituals with respect.

In 1936 Schultes was a young Harvard undergraduate, studying botany. After the chance reading of an academic paper about an obscure hallucinogenic cactus called peyote, he became obsessed and chose to write his undergraduate thesis on this plant. Despite his age and inexperience, Schultes believed in a 'hands on' approach to his research and – with his tutor's blessing and funding – made a 1,400-mile (2,250-km) journey from Boston to Oklahoma to live with and study a peyote cult practiced by the Kiowa people. White settlers had long since taken their land and suppressed their customs, so the Kiowa were understandably wary of Schultes, but he won them over by his reverence, humility and desire to learn, and was eventually invited to partake in a peyote ceremony.

The vivid colours and powerful visions induced by the plant were like nothing he'd experienced before. Schultes ended up staying for two months with the Kiowa, ingesting peyote four times a week. Through his experiences and observations he came to see that peyote was non-addictive, had no side-effects and was in fact medicine, used for psychological and physical healing. He even witnessed it being given to members of the community who had succumbed to drink or drug problems, to help rid themselves of destructive behaviours. But while prohibition of alcohol had recently been lifted in mid-1930s USA, peyote ceremonies, such as those conducted by the

Top left Dr Richard Evan Schultes in the Amazon. **Above** Members of the Kiowa indigenous people of the Great Plains, in their summer attire. **Left** A peyote ceremony in 1892.

The peyote cactus is known for its psychoactive properties when ingested, and has a long history of ritualistic and medicinal use by indigenous North Americans.

Kiowa, were still illegal and hidden. After returning to Harvard, Schultes travelled to Washington, DC. Despite being just a 21-year-old undergraduate, he successfully testified to Congress for the rights of the Kiowa (and others) to conduct their sacred peyote ceremonies.

THIS WAS ONLY the beginning of Schultes's exotic travels. Immersed in further research at Washington's Smithsonian Institute of Natural History, he came across a letter which referenced a semi-mythical mushroom, teonánacatl, once believed to have been used in rituals by Aztecs priests. It was widely believed that teonánacatl and peyote were one and the same, but Schultes now knew that peyote was a cactus, not a fungi. With support and funding again from his liberal-minded tutor, Schultes headed off on his next adventure, deep into Mexico in search of the legendary teonanácatl.

This time his travels combined long, dusty Greyhound bus rides, teeth-rattling trains and buttock-numbing journeys on horseback before he reached his destination – a tiny village occupied by the Mazatek people of Oaxaca in the southern mountains of Mexico. During one of his interminably long bus journeys, Schultes came to realize the limitations of his Spanish when, intending to enquire about her age, he inadvertently asked an old lady how many arseholes she had. Surprised, the *anciana* replied: 'I've only got the one. Why, how many do white men have?'

Schultes wasn't alone for this trip. Accompanying him was an Austrian-born but now local botanist, Blas Pablo Reko, an essential guide but – to Schultes's dismay – also an ardent Nazi sympathizer. In Oaxaca, the pair met another team searching for the elusive teonánacatl, led by Bernard Bevan, whom Schultes discovered to be working for the British secret service. As early as the 1930s, natural hallucinogenics were already being sought out by intelligence agencies, intent on discovering whether they could be used for brainwashing enemy spies.

After weeks of searching, Schultes located the sacred mushrooms, witnessed their use in sacred ceremonies and noted that, as with the Kiowa, the Mazatek were using teonánacatl as medicine for the body and mind. Like the Kiowa, too, they believed their sacred medicine to be possessed by spirits ('little gods') who taught the shamans how to help them heal the sick. By travelling into previously unchartered territory with an open mind to Mazatec practices and rituals, Schultes was unearthing an aspect to indigenous culture that had, up until then, been ignored, outlawed or suppressed by white settlers as dangerous hokum.

BY 1941, with war raging across Europe, Schultes found himself in demand as an ethnobotanist by the US government, and was offered a ten-month grant to locate the botanical sources of curare – the poison used in blow darts – in the hope that it would help victims of the war. Curare's paralysing properties had long been known about, and its application as a muscle relaxant would prove to be revolutionary in the science of anaesthesia. In the mid-20th century, however, the botanical sources of curare were still unknown.

Ten months for Schultes turned out to be 13 virtually uninterrupted years. He travelled through Columbia on foot, over the Andes and into the north-west Amazon – a remote area equivalent in size to Germany and one of the last unexplored places on the planet. For many of the indigenous people he encountered, Schultes was the first white man they'd ever seen.

Along with the secrets of curare, Schultes was also on the lookout for new hallucinogens, and in 1942 in Ecuador he spent time living with the Cofan people, whose 'vine of the soul', ayahuasca, is now considered to be the most powerful hallucinogenic in the world. Naturally, Schultes participated in ayahuasca ceremonies, experiencing complex patterns, visions and telepathy. Once again, he encountered the belief that within these plants resided spirits.

'In these parts of the world there is no concept of organically caused sickness. It is all caused by the invisible arrows of malevolent spirits. The medicine man converses with these spirits and can diagnose the illness and affect a cure.'
American Academy of Achievement, interview with Richard Schultes, 1990

Another curious aspect of ayahuasca is the common conviction of the *ayahuasqueros* (medicine men or women) that the plant takes experienced users to the microcosmic world. Fifty years after Schultes's research, Canadian anthropologist James Narby would write about his own experiences with ayahuasca in the Amazon. His book *The Cosmic Serpent* put forward the hypothesis that ayahuasca actually provides a 'microscope' for looking at the quantum world, and that DNA has been understood for thousands of years by some of the indigenous cultures of the Amazon, symbolized in their art by entwined twin serpents, a motif also found in other cultures, such as the caduceus (staff of Hermes) in Greek mythology.

DURING HIS 13 years' travelling through the Amazon, Schultes sported a pith helmet, moccasins, a camera and machete, and carried just one change of clothes. He refused to carry a gun, asserting that all indigenous people are friendly if approached with the right degree of respect. The only food he carried with him was instant coffee and tins of beans, relying almost entirely on the kindness of strangers.

While fearless and trailblazing, Schultes was not immune to the sometimes treacherous nature of the Amazon's environment and came close to death several times. He was bitten by vampire bats, contracted malaria 24 times, and in September 1943 had been incommunicado with the outside world for so long that he was presumed dead.

In 1947, travelling down the Rio Negro in a remote part of Brazil, Schultes began to notice a tingling and numbness in his hands and feet, and realized, to his horror, that he had contracted beriberi, a potentially fatal disease caused by vitamin deficiency. He badly needed a vitamin injection, but the nearest city, Manaus, was over a thousand miles away.

Gradually losing feeling in his extremities, he walked for four weeks with the aid of sticks to a military outpost in the hope of getting a plane to Manaus, only to discover there was no plane. For another month he travelled downriver. At one point his canoe capsized and he lost all his supplies and specimens. True to form, when Schultes then encountered an unknown tribe whose sacred hallucinogen plant was unfamiliar to him, despite being close to death he took part in their sacred ceremony and went off the next day in search of the plant. After another month of extreme discomfort, exhaustion and lack of food he reached Manaus and received the life-saving injection. Ignoring the advice of his doctors, three days later he was back in the jungle.

Schultes is often cited as the godfather of ethnobotany. He collected over 30,000 plant species from South America and uncovered some of the botanical secrets of curare, peyote, magic mushrooms and ayahuasca, to name but a few. He remained in South America until 1953, sourcing new rubber plantations for the US government at a time when the West's rubber resources were becoming perilously low.

From then on, he became a full-time lecturer at Harvard, delighting students with his blow-dart demonstrations in class and leaving a bucket of peyote buttons outside his lecture room as 'an optional laboratory experiment'. His name became something of a password in the Amazon for anyone who, following in his footsteps, needed to gain the trust of any indigenous tribes that Schultes had met. He was, according to his biographer, Wade Davis, a 'real-life Indiana Jones'.

During his lifetime Schultes would have a mountain, 2.2 million acres (890,000 ha) of protected rainforest, 120 species of Amazonian plants and even a cockroach named after him. He was not without his eccentricities either. Schultes didn't subscribe to the American Revolution and during election times he opted to cross out the names of all American presidential candidates on the ballot paper and replace them with the word 'queen'. A colleague once commented that the only way Schultes could go truly native would be to move to London.

Gordon Wasson 1898–1986

Schultes never anticipated (or welcomed) the psychedelic revolution that was to follow in his wake. But while his published papers were not widely read, the one detailing his experiences with the teonánacatl mushroom in Mexico reached the attention of author and poet Robert Graves in the 1940s, who passed it on to a friend, R. Gordon Wasson.

As vice-president of a US investment banking company, Wasson cut an unlikely figure as seeker and psychonaut, yet he and his wife had devoted 30 years to researching and documenting mushroom cults across the globe. How Wasson came to be fascinated with sacred mushrooms is curious in itself. In 1927, having recently married a Russian paediatrician, Valentina Pavlovna Guercken, Wasson discovered on

Schultes is often cited as the godfather of ethnobotany. He collected over 30,000 plant species from South America and uncovered some of the botanical secrets of curare, peyote, magic mushrooms (*pictured*) and ayahuasca.

a trip to the Catskill Mountains that his wife was a mycophile – she had an intense passion for fungi. He would later write, jokingly: 'Like all good Anglo-Saxons, I knew nothing about the fungal world and felt that the less I knew about those putrid, treacherous excrescences the better' (*Life*, 10 June, 1957).

In truth, he was determined not to let this 'minor difference' get between them, so together they became amateur mycologists. What they discovered surprised them both – fungi belong to neither the plant or animal world but are considered to be an entirely independent kingdom. They appear in the artwork, myths and legends of many cultures, with magic mushroom and toadstool-worshipping cults having once existed across the globe, from Russia and Catalonia to South America.

The Wassons' extensive research uncovered a recurring legend across myriad cultures – that sacred mushrooms were procreated by lightning bolts from the heavens. This was believed by the Māori of New Zealand and the Zapotecs of Mexico. It was in the myths of ancient Greece, Rome, India, Persia, Tibet, China and the Philippines. Why were fungi thought to have been sent from the heavens?

Fifty years after the Wassons' discovery, astrobiologists have begun to theorize that fungi spores might conceivably have arrived on our planet from elsewhere, following the discovery that some spores are able to survive the harsh environment of deep space. If fungi really did arrive on Earth by meteor, could the thunderbolt myth be some form of trace memory? Others have proffered even wilder theories that magic mushrooms and other organic psychedelics may have accelerated or even triggered human consciousness.

AFTER READING of Schultes's experiences with the teonánacatl mushroom, in 1955 the Wassons set off to the remote Mixeteco mountains of southern Mexico in search of their own 'final fix'. They would go on to spend four consecutive summers there (the risk of malaria was too high in other seasons), gaining the trust of the Mazatek and finally partaking in the mushroom ceremonies that Schultes had uncovered.

As with Schultes 20 years previously, teonánacatl also attracted the interest of intelligence agencies. Unbeknown to Wasson, the CIA sent an undercover representative and chemist with him to Mexico during one of his visits, intent on gaining the secrets of the magic mushroom in order to create a drug that could be used to control people. When LSD emerged, the CIA turned its attention to that drug instead, testing it on unsuspecting members of the public and the armed forces, with disastrous consequences.

In 1957 Gordon Wasson agreed to write an essay about one of his trips for *Life* magazine. Entitled 'Seeking the Magic Mushroom', the subheading ran: 'A New York banker goes to Mexico's mountains to participate in the age-old rituals of Indians who chew strange growths that produce visions.' The magazine declared the Wassons to be the first white people in recorded history to take part in sacred mushroom ceremonies. They were accompanied by *Life* photographer Allan Richardson, who had promised faithfully to his wife that he would document the rituals but not participate. When push came to shove the promise evaporated, with Richardson muttering, 'My God, what will Mary say?' as he began ingesting the sacred fungi.

The ceremony was led by mother and daughter *curanderas* – medicine women – who led the ritual and danced, sung and chanted until 4am, when the effects began to wear off. Wasson wrote:

After half an hour the vision came … in vivid colors, always harmonious. They began with art motifs … then evolved into places with courts, arcades and gardens. Later I was suspended in mid-air viewing landscapes of mountains.
'Seeking the Magic Mushroom'

Deeper still into the hallucinations he confessed:

I was seeing the archetypes, the Platonic ideas that underlie the imperfect images of everyday life … For the first time the word ecstasy took on real meaning. For the first time it did not mean someone else's state of mind.
'Seeking the Magic Mushroom'

Whereas Schultes's papers on peyote and teonánacatl were mainly read and circulated by a small academic elite, Wesson's essay in *Life* magazine was read by millions. One such was a Harvard researcher called Timothy Leary who headed straight to Mexico to take part in a mushroom ceremony himself, after reading it.

Slowly and surely, this small village in the Mixeteco mountains began to find itself inundated with psychedelic tourists, wishing to experience the ecstasy, astral travel and vivid colours that Wasson had so eloquently described. John Lennon, Bob Dylan and Keith Richards were among many of its pilgrims. An unintentional and unhappy consequence of this saw traditional life in the village destroyed by the growing influx of seekers. Many were disrespectful of its traditions, bringing pot, alcohol and other drugs to the village, while the doors were now opened for less scrupulous medicine men and women to exploit these visitors. Pretty soon the dedicated psychonauts would need to journey even further afield for the 'authentic' psychedelic experience. And, like Burroughs, they would go looking for 'the final fix'.

IN THE 1960s LSD, a synthetic hallucinogenic, with similar chemical compounds to teonánacatl, became widely available for anyone wishing to experience a psychedelic trip. It became the defining mind-expanding drug of the counterculture, taken by millions and reaching its zenith in the late 1960s with the Summer of Love, at Woodstock, and the rapscallion Dr Timothy Leary urging the counterculture to 'tune in, turn on, drop out'.

Schultes wanted no part in the psychedelic revolution; he believed that taking mind-altering drugs without the necessary rituals and guides was reckless and dangerous. But LSD did not curtail the interest in psychedelic pilgrimages. In 1968 Carlos Castaneda, a mysterious anthropologist from the University of California, Los Angeles (UCLA) wrote *The Teachings of Don Juan*, in which he claimed to have met a Native American medicine man in Arizona in the early 1960s, who taught him the secrets of peyote. For the hippy generation, Castenada popularized the idea of a more authentic approach to taking psychedelics and a pilgrimage in search of 'the final fix'. That the authenticity of Castaneda's book was itself soon cast into doubt was unimportant to a new legion of fans, hungry to experience such quests. *The Teachings of Don Juan* became a global bestseller, spawning further books. In 1973 *Time* magazine called Castaneda, 'an enigma wrapped in a mystery, wrapped in a tortilla'.

Terence McKenna 1946–2000

In 1971, inspired by Castenda, Wasson and Schultes, and after extensive travels through Asia and the Middle East, a graduate named Terence McKenna, together with his brother Dennis, also journeyed into the Amazon in search of hallucinogens.

We were graduates of the LSD revolution but it left us wanting more, specifically the kind of experiences and visions the classical commentators described.
Terence McKenna, True Hallucinations, *1993*

After participating in a mushroom ceremony McKenna claimed to experience 'pure understanding', while his brother Dennis came to the startling realization that, through these rituals, it was possible to give birth to one's soul as a physical organ. Dennis carefully prepared for this 'psychic reversal', performed the experiment during a mushroom ritual and 'promptly went bananas' (*True Hallucinations*).

While Dennis's experiences serve as a reminder of the potential dangers of dabbling with psychotropics, by the 1990s Terence had become the voice of a new generation of psychonauts. A versatile public speaker, he travelled the world eulogizing about sacred plants, speaking at festivals, and even being sampled by acid house and rave DJs.

In his most popular book, *Food of the Gods*, McKenna put forward the hypothesis that human consciousness may have been accelerated or even triggered by our ancestors' first contact with hallucinogens. And those fungi, in turn, just might have arrived here from deep space – Wasson's 'flash of lightning'.

In man's evolutionary past, as he groped his way out from his lowly past, there must have come a moment in time when he discovered the secret of the hallucinatory mushrooms. Their effect on him, as I see it, could only have been profound, a detonator to new ideas.
Gordon Wasson, 'Seeking the Magic Mushroom'

Unlike Leary and Burroughs, McKenna got the blessing from the godfather of ethnobotany Richard Evans Schultes, who, in reviewing *Food of the Gods* described it as 'a masterpiece of research and writing', and said that it should 'be read by every specialist working in the multifarious fields involved with the use of psychoactive drugs' (*American Scientist*, 1993).

NOWADAYS A NEW kind of tourism is booming in South America: ayahuasca retreats. Participating in sacred plant ceremonies has become something of a rite of passage for the New Age tourist, sending the price of the *Banisteriopsis caapi* vine – the raw ingredient in ayahuasca – spiralling in recent years. It has even become a popular theme for alternative travel programmes, with presenters journeying to Peru, Ecuador and Columbia to sample ayahuasca and candidly describing their visions on camera. As with the tourist invasion of Mixeteco in the 1950s and 1960s, this has come at a price to the indigenous people.

Understandably, however, the potentially healing properties of these plants continue

In the 1960s LSD became widely available and was the defining mind-expanding drug of the counterculture. Taken by millions, it reached its zenith in the late 1960s with the Summer of Love, at Woodstock (pictured).

Terence McKenna put forward the hypothesis that human consciousness may have been accelerated or even triggered by our ancestors' first contact with hallucinogens.

to fascinate people in the West. In 2005 *National Geographic* journalist Kira Salak wrote of her experiences using ayahuasca to overcome a long and debilitating struggle with depression. It remains the most popular article the magazine has ever published. Conferences and events themed around sacred plants are on the rise, too, from the Ayahuasca Monologues in New York to Breaking Conventions in the UK.

Despite nascent scientific evidence that these substances may have the power to heal addictions and potentially play a role in slowing down degenerative diseases such as Parkinson's and Alzheimer's, they remain illegal across most parts of the world.

As we edge ever closer to cutting-edge VR technology being affordable in our own homes, soon we won't even have to leave our homes to immerse ourselves in alternative 360-degree realms. Yet will such experiences, deprived of context and truly artificial, ever be 'true hallucinations' or true journeys of consciousness? For growing numbers of seekers, many of them willing to travel halfway across the world, the chance to experience virtual worlds of our own creation – which hold the alleged potential to heal and even transform perception – remains the ultimate journey; the final fix. *DB*

Book
The Yage Letters, William Burroughs and Allen Ginsberg (City Lights Books, 1963)
A collection of correspondence and experimental writings by Beat Generation authors William S. Burroughs and Allen Ginsberg.

One River: Explorations and Discoveries in the Amazon Rain Forest, Wade Davis (Vintage, 1996)
The definitive story of Schultes's life.

Food of the Gods: The Search for the Original Tree of Knowledge: A Radical History of Plants, Drugs and Human Evolution, Terence McKenna (Rider, 1999)
A journey to some of the Earth's most endangered people in the remote Upper Amazon, an examination of rituals in the Bwiti cults of Gabon and Zaire and an investigation into the eating habits of 'stoned' apes and chimpanzees: all this and more in ethnobotanist Terence McKenna's extraordinary quest to discover the fruit of the Tree of Knowledge.

Film
Embrace of the Serpent (dir. Ciro Guerra, 2015)
A film inspired by the travel journals of Theodor Koch-Grunberg and Richard Evans Schultes, and dedicated to lost Amazonian cultures.

Article
'Seeking the Magic Mushroom', R. Gordon Wasson (*Life* magazine, 10 June, 1957)
A New York banker goes to Mexico's mountains to participate in the age-old rituals of Indians who chew strange fungi that produce visions. Full article: imaginaria.org/wasson/life.htm

Unexpected odysseys
of body parts

Adolf Hitler's jaw: alleged travels of the Führer's bones | Napoleon Bonaparte:
the fateful journey of 'Boney's item' | The bishop of Patara: the lost bones of Santa
Claus | Grigori Rasputin: the missing parts of Russia's greatest love machine

Sometimes, bits of historic figures live on long after the rest of them has turned to dust. You've no doubt heard of holy relics – St John's head, Jesus' foreskin – but what about the less than holy ones?

Adolf Hitler 1889–1945

The journey of Adolf Hitler's bones, and their final resting place, is a hotly contested one. Stalin was keen to make sure that he had them, excavating the Berlin bomb crater where Hitler's remains were supposedly buried on numerous occasions. At first, the KGB thought it had found them, displaying the Führer's burnt corpse for two days until it was discovered to be a double.

They also kept a skull fragment and jaw bone unearthed in a later dig. In 1946 Hitler's dentist had confirmed that the bones were his, but over the succeeding years the Kremlin put out so much disinformation concerning the whereabouts of Hitler's body and the nature of his death that it's difficult to prove any single version – and when scientists finally got their hands on the fragments in 2009, DNA testing showed that the skull had belonged to a woman.

The case is made muddier by the fact that nobody apparently witnessed Hitler's suicide, only the immediate aftermath, and so reports of his escape and long life in Argentina also began to flourish. It all started in 1946 when Stalin claimed, when quizzed by President Truman, that Hitler was still alive.

In 1945 the Allies tasked British intelligence officer Hugh Trevor-Roper with finally

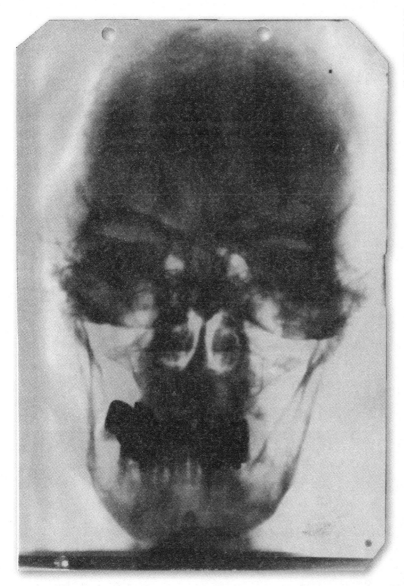

One of five known X-rays of Hitler's head, part of his medical records compiled by American military intelligence after Germany declassified them in 1958.

getting to the bottom of things. Trevor-Roper concluded that Hitler had indeed died in his bunker and his remains had been seized by the KGB. The conventional wisdom since is that Hitler and his long-term companion Eva Braun were repeatedly buried and exhumed by SMERSH (the KGB's anti-spy unit) during their relocation from Berlin to Magdeburg. The bodies, along with those of the Nazi Minister of Propaganda

Joseph Goebbels and his family, were buried in an unmarked grave beneath the front courtyard. On 4 April 1970, fearing the location becoming known and treated as a site of pilgrimage for the Far Right, Russia's then-leader, Yuri Andropov, ordered the bones to be dug up and burned and the ashes thrown into the Elbe.

None of this has stopped the History Channel making three series of *Hunting Hitler*, based on investigations from leads found in recently declassified CIA and FBI files. Stories of huge Nazi bases existing in the Argentinian jungle, with many witnesses claiming to have spent time with the Hitlers may be tantalizing but they remain in the realm of conspiracy theory.

Napoleon Bonaparte 1769–1821

As we leave one European dictator's remains flowing down the Elbe, another – Napoleon Bonaparte – rears his head or, rather, his genitals. Bonaparte's penis – all 1½ inches (3.8 cm) of it apparently – is currently in the possession of one Evan Lattimer of New Jersey, who inherited it from his father, a urologist who bought it in an auction in Paris for $3,000. The artefact is known euphemistically within the Lattimer family as 'Napoleon's Item', and the current owner has only ever shown it to ten people.

After being removed in front of 17 witnesses by Napoleon's personal doctor, Francesco Autommarchi, Bonaparte's part was preserved and has passed through many hands. Italian priest Abbé Ange Paul Vignali, who gave the leader his last rites, was the first owner. It then passed down through Vignali's family before it was eventually bought by American rare books dealer A. S. W. Rosenbach in 1924; next it went to a London bookseller, then another in Philadelphia, before being displayed

Right Goyathlay, later known as Geronimo ('the one who yawns'), Chief of the Chiricahua Apaches, 1890. His skull is rumoured to still be used as a drinking cup in ceremonies by the Skull and Bones Society at Yale University.

Opposite Portrait of Napoleon in his forties, in high-ranking white and dark-blue military dress uniform. The current owner of his 'item' has apparently only ever shown it to ten people.

St Nicholas of Bari –
a third-century Turkish
bishop of Patara – was
the original Saint Nick
whose bones have
been scattered around
the world.

at the Museum of French Art in New York in 1927. Why booksellers seemed to have such interest in the imperial penis is unclear. Napoleon may have ridden roughshod over most of Europe, but the most intimate part of his mortal remains is now even better travelled than when attached to him.

THE INDIGNITIES AND odysseys endured by iconic people's body parts seem almost endemic: Albert Einstein's and Benito Mussolini's brains have been scooped, sliced, sold, stolen, smuggled, swapped and displayed. The skull of Geronimo – former leader of the Chiricahua Apache tribe – is rumoured to be used as a drinking cup in ceremonies by the Skull and Bones Society at Yale (most US Presidents have apparently drunk out of the skull; understandably his tribe is suing the government to get it back). Anne Boleyn's heart was torn out, only to be secretly preserved by Henry VIII and then discovered in the wall of a church in Suffolk. Tom Paine's bones ended up in a box in William Cobbett's attic before being turned into buttons. Can there be any greater outrage to our sensibilities, however, than pirates raiding the tomb of Father Christmas, and stealing his bones? (Spoiler for any kids reading; yes, we're afraid he is dead.)

Saint Nicholas 270–343

Nicholas of Bari, a third-century Turkish bishop of Patara, was the original Saint Nick. He inherited big from his parents, but instead of becoming a property developer he gave it all away anonymously in order to alleviate social ills. One of his good works was throwing gold coins through the open windows of houses where parents didn't have a dowry for their daughters, thus preventing them from being sold into prostitution – hence the tradition of giving chocolate coins at Christmas.

The saint's body was enshrined in the church of St Nicholas in Demre, Turkey, for 600-odd years until 1087 when Italian pirates raided the church and stole the bones (or saved them from Moorish invaders, depending on your point of view). They did the decent thing and took them for safekeeping to a dedicated shrine in Bari, Italy. Five hundred bone fragments had been left behind, however, so later Crusaders went back to the town and seized them, taking the holy relics back for safekeeping in Venice.

Most of what is left of Saint Nick can be found in these two places, Bari and Venice, but remember that this is Father Christmas – a pretty popular guy – so bits of his bones can be found in reliquaries in France, Germany and the USA; there's also a finger bone along with a treasure trove in Quebec and a pelvic bone in Morton Grove, Illinois. A Father O'Neill of Chicago also claims to have obtained his pubic bone – via a Belgian smuggler and a trove of hidden relics from the French Revolution – and he has the carbon dating evidence to prove it. It seems this Santa really does get everywhere.

However, in October 2017 Turkish archaeologists using ground-penetrating radar uncovered a previously unknown and undamaged cavity underneath the church of St Nicholas. Excavations are imminent. Could it be that Saint Nick was under the floorboards all along?

Grigori Rasputin 1869–1916

The single most mysterious and extraordinary posthumous odyssey, however, belongs to an unholy relic of the man some considered to be the Antichrist. Many legends surround the pilgrim, mystic and faith-healer Grigori Rasputin, one-time advisor to the Romanov family and, as Boney M famously put it, 'Russia's greatest love machine'. Of all the famous fables, few are quite as long-winded, or amusing, as the stories directly concerned with the Mad Monk's gigantic genitalia.

Since Rasputin's assassination in 1916 many people have claimed to own the Siberian's penis, with one prominent Russian doctor currently displaying what he upholds as the real McCoy in his Museum of Erotica in St Petersburg. At 11 inches (28 cm), you can see why the wife of the Czar was one of many interested parties; Rasputin was a shower not a grower.

Rasputin parted company with his 'old chap' shortly after his assassination, it being chopped off by a group of jealous noblemen who'd no doubt had just about enough of the unfavourable comparisons made by wives and mistresses. It was left at the scene until, legend has it, an enterprising housemaid slipped it into her sock and stole away with it. It next reared its head in the 1920s, when a group of Russian women living in Paris got hold of what they thought was Rasputin's penis and worshipped it as a kind of holy relic, while keeping it in a wooden casket. Rasputin's daughter Maria, meanwhile, got wind of this and demanded that they hand it back. 'Give me back my dad's penis!' is a sentence no woman should ever have to utter.

The artefact remained with Maria, enjoying a well-earned retirement, until her death in 1977. It then disappeared for some time, popping up in 1993 in the hands of a Californian named Michael Augustine, who found it slipped into a velvet pouch next to some of Maria Rasputin's manuscripts. Augustine had purchased the items from a certain Dr Roberta Ripple shortly after Rasputin's daughter had died. Ripple had worked with Maria Rasputin on a biography of her father, and so had allegedly inherited the member after the daughter's death.

Augustine sold the well-travelled penis to Bonham's Fine Art Auctioneers, who had it tested for authenticity. Bonham's discovered that what they had bought was not a penis but a dehydrated sea cucumber. A very expensive sea cucumber.

That should have been the end of the story but then in 2014, out of the blue, Rasputin's penis was splashed all over the media once again. The Russian Museum of

Grigori Rasputin: pilgrim, mystic, faith-healer, one-time advisor to the Romanov family and, as Boney M famously put it, 'Russia's greatest love machine'.

Erotica was claiming that it had the penis. Igor Knyazkin, director of the museum and head physician of the Prostate Centre of Russia's Academy of Sciences, claimed that he had bought it from a French antiquarian for $8,000 who had it on good authority that the emigré ladies of Paris (the ones who had revered the penis as a holy relic) had fobbed Maria off with a sea cucumber, keeping the real deal for themselves. It's likely, however, that the one being displayed is a cleverly adapted horse penis. One might also ponder why the museum's penis is preserved in fluid, whereas all early accounts of Rasputin's penis describe it as being dried. But, as Knyazkin has forbidden any kind of DNA testing, we won't be discovering the truth any time soon.

Rasputin's reputation is currently undergoing a rehabilitation back in Mother

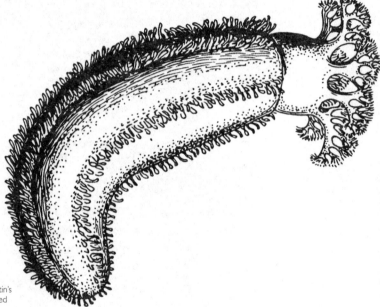

Somewhere along the way, Rasputin's penis was replaced by a dehydrated sea cucumber.

Russia. In December 1996 Vladimir Osipov, a writer and monarchist, organized a requiem to Rasputin in a church in Moscow to mark the 80th anniversary of his assassination, and has regular conferences about the not-as-naughty-as-previously-thought monk. The stories about Rasputin being a drunk and a womanizer are, according to Osipov, 'complete lies, perpetrated by historians whose only sources were falsifications published at the time by anti-monarchists trying to bring down the Romanovs'. So there we are. Ra Ra Rasputin, a lovely man who loved the Queen. DM

TV Programme
Hunting Hitler (History Channel, 2015)
Investigative TV series based on the hypothetical premise that, if Adolf Hitler had escaped from the Führerbunker in Berlin at the end of the Second World War, how he would have done it and where he would be now.

Dead Famous DNA (All 4, 2014)
Host Mark Evans investigates whether the DNA extracted from the remains of infamous historical figures (such as a strand of Eva Braun's hair) can add to their biographies.

Book
Rasputin: A Short Life, Frances Welch (Atria Books, 2014)
This humorous biography delves into the bizarre story of Grigori Rasputin's close relationship with the Romanov dynasty, and how the Siberian peasant-turned-holy man managed to nestle himself into the Russian royal family while bedding thousands of women and getting wasted several nights a week.

The Dadaist journeyman

Andrew Kötting: the film-maker who travelled
with an inflatable 'deadad'

Through epic walks, open-water swimming and completing the Channel I'm confronting goals that other people might not achieve. I see it as an act of mild heroism. Isn't everyone struggling for recognition? And by bringing in Dadaism, there's an element of undermining oneself, ultimately parodying the act itself. It's a very British quality.
Andrew Kötting in interview with David Bramwell, March 2018

Early morning in late summer 2011, three drunken sailors set out from Hastings, UK, in a stolen vessel and set a course for France. Their plan – to undertake a booze cruise – was destined to go awry. Their singular choice of seafaring vehicle was a pedalo swan, stolen from a seafront amusement park.

The trio managed less than a mile before being reported to the police, forced to return to shore and offer their sincere apologies to the owner of the pedalo. Most onlookers blamed the theft on drunken bravado. However, it's possible the thieves' motivation came from a different source: an earlier sighting of two other men out at sea on a pedalo swan, one of them dressed in a suit and tie. This pair, author Iain Sinclair and rogue film-maker and artist Andrew Kötting, got considerably further than the sailors: a 200-mile (320-km) journey designed to test their calf muscles and resilience.

The original premise for a shared watery journey came about when psycho-geographer Sinclair first asked Kötting – a keen swimmer – to swim around his home turf of Hackney. 'Swim up the murky River Lea into the labyrinthine canal system,' Sinclair had suggested. Kötting was less than keen; London's waterways are still rather polluted. Looking out of his Hastings studio window one day, however, Kötting's eyes fell on the collection of pedalo swans bobbing in the amusement park lake and the idea for a very different journey was set.

For the first few days Kötting and Sinclair were prevented from leaving by rough seas, until a libation (a cheap bottle of wine) was offered to Neptune and the storm abated. Contrary to all professional advice, they remained at sea for three days, pedalling from Hastings to Rye before heading inland 80 miles (129 km) down the River Rother and Kent's Royal Military Canal, up the Medway to the Thames and into the heart of East London. For Sinclair, the journey was a protest against the 'militarization' of his beloved Hackney by the developments for the London Olympics. For Kötting, it was a wilful act of Dada.

> It was about serendipity and the physical impossibility of hauling a large swan-shaped object up riverbanks and across muddy fields. It was about spending a whole month in the same clothes and being able to wet myself whenever I wanted to. Kötting in Swandown *(dir. Andrew Kötting, 2012)*

The pedalo – named after King Harold's handfast maiden Edith Swan-Neck – constantly leaked, leading Kötting to contract trench-foot from an infection in his leg. Accompanying them was another swan – a plastic decoy – which the two men had first taken on an earlier 200-mile (320-km) journey by foot, in preparation for the pedalo.

Pedalo swans at Flamingo Park in Hastings.

According to Kötting, Herzog's *Fitzcarraldo* was part-inspiration for peddling an 'awkward plastic swan' 200 miles (320 km) from the English Channel into the heart of London.

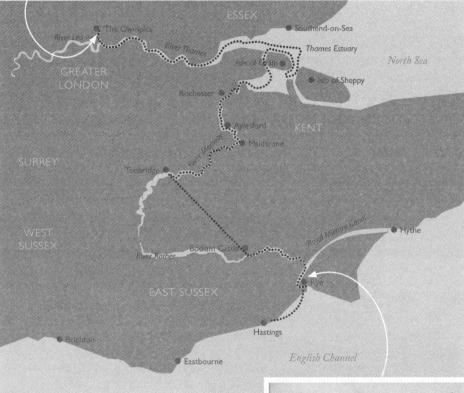

ESSEX

River Lea   The Olympics   Southend-on-Sea

River Thames   Thames Estuary

GREATER LONDON   Isle of Grain   North Sea

Isle of Sheppy

Rochester

SURREY   Aylesford   KENT

Maidstone

River Medway

Tonbridge

WEST SUSSEX   Hythe

Royal Military Canal

River Rother   Bodiam Castle

EAST SUSSEX   Rye

Hastings

Brighton

Eastbourne   English Channel

Above The original plan for an unbroken water journey along the River Rother and up to Tonbridge was shortened by an overland detour.

Right Contrary to all professional advice, Kötting and Sinclair pedalled at sea for three days, travelling from Hastings to Rye (*pictured, right*).

THE DADAIST JOURNEYMAN   **167**

Near the end of their watery travels Sinclair was required to head off for a writing residency in the USA, leaving Kötting in a very lopsided pedalo, getting ever closer to the building sites of the Olympics. He was finally warned off by security guards with the menacing and surreal shout of 'Keep away from the Olympics', as if it was a physical entity.

Kötting and Sinclair catalogued their journey through words, maps, photos and a film, *Swandown* (2012). The adventure may have connected their respective homes and carried a political agenda for Sinclair, but two men in a pedalo swan was ultimately a journey entrenched in endurance and absurdity, typical of Kötting's preferred brand of travel.

KÖTTING IS a restless journeyman, adventurer and mischief-maker. Unlike many of our great travel writers, his are not lone journeys into the heart of the unknown; they are communal and familial, fed by happenstance and the folk he meets. These are modern-day pilgrimages in which Kötting collects people along the way, like the Pied Piper.

Kötting's seven-year-old daughter, Eden, and his grandmother, Gladys, during the filming of *Gallivant*.

From garden gnomes to rubber rings:
Kötting's memory map from *Gallivant*, his
2006 tour of the entire coastline of Britain
with his seven-year-old daughter, Eden,
and his grandmother, Gladys.

The Hill of Many Stones
Language   dialect
The Old Man   John
of Hoy   O'Groats
Carnival   Toby
Short wave radio   Jugs
Collage   Sub-codes
Hebrides   Golf
Rising more slowly   Poetic   Plus-fours
Garden gnomes   Discursive Structures   Clava Cairns
Fortean Times   Chance
Sunless   Mosey
Crusty   Prance
Hoi Polloi   Quest
Primitive   Bus   Sex
Shelters   Bowling
Pavilions   Green
Odyssey   Broadcast
Cairn   Context
Liath Broch   Arbroath
Rock   Allotments   Coast
T.V.   Poppy   Guard
Quest   Day   Area
Gobstopper   Scotch Eggs   of
M.O.T.s   Outstanding
Lollypop ladies   Natural
Gatehouse of Fleet   Beauty
Mystical Thematic Threads   Castles
Cheese rolling   Birds
Cricket pitch   Sub-aqua
Rubber rings   Cliffs
Folklore   Heritage
The Lake District   Religion
Rediffusion   Mix-ups
Super 8   Evasion
Chaos   of imposed
Piers   and finite
Connections and Reveals   meaning
Semiotics   Grotesque
Public Houses   Realism   Circumstances of
Ancient   sites   Inquisitive   Utterance
Caravans   Pot-pourri
Travel   Priests
Pagan   Gypsies
Tattooing   Vagabonds
Amusement arcades   Salvation
Hunt the thimble   Army
Maypole   Hare
Milkman   and
D.A.T.   Ice Cream   tortoise
Morris Dancers   Punch   Bucket
and   Severn   and
Judy   Bridge   spade
99s   Mnemonics   Guide dogs for the blind
Samples   Life
Jumble   Boat
Sales   Men
Off license   Jarman's Garden
Paper boy   De La War Pavilion, Bexhill on Sea
Pickled eggs   Juxtaposition, funny ha-ha
Weston super   deck chair
Mare   post modernism
Lands light fishing boat   chalet
End   house   metaphor

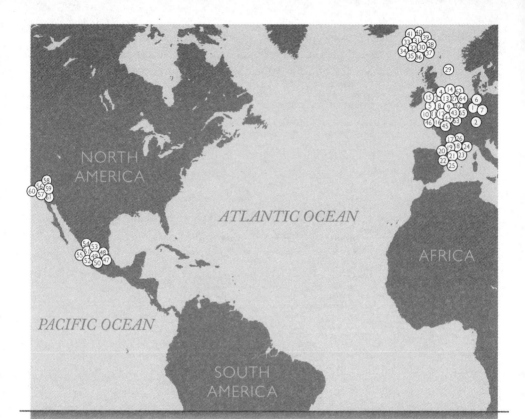

THE 65 INFLATION SITES OF DEADAD

1. Wuppertal, GERMANY
2. Buch, GERMANY
3. Highgate, London, UK
4. Sidcup, Kent, UK
5. Regents Street, London, UK
6. Schebebahn, Wuppertal, GERMANY
7. Huppertsburg Factory, GERMANY
8. St Nicholas, Church, Kent, UK
9. St John's Church, Sidcup, Kent, UK
10. Morköt, Elmstead Woods, Kent, UK
11. Morköt, Elmstead Woods, Kent, UK
12. Morköt, Elmstead Woods, Kent, UK
13. Evelyn Street, London, UK
14. Bench House, Pepys Estate, London, UK
15. Stave Hill, Surrey Docks, London, UK
16. Hastings Beach, East Sussex, UK
17. Les Moureous, Ariège, FRANCE
18. Montségur, Ariège, FRANCE
19. Montségur, Ariège, FRANCE
20. Louyre, Ariège, FRANCE
21. Louyre, Ariège, FRANCE
22. Louyre, Ariège, FRANCE
23. Forest, French Pyrenees
24. Louyre, Ariège, FRANCE
25. Louyre, Ariège, FRANCE
26. Louyre, Ariège, FRANCE
27. Longlands Road, Kent, UK
28. N/A
29. Somewhere in the NORTH SEA
30. FAROE ISLANDS
31. Tjørnuvík, FAROE ISLANDS
32. Tórshavn, FAROE ISLANDS
33. Vagar, FAROE ISLANDS
34. Red Church, Sandvags, FAROE IS.
35. Streymoy, FAROE ISLANDS
36. East coast, Streymoy, FAROE IS.
37. West coast, Streymoy, FAROE IS.
38. Streymoy, FAROE ISLANDS
39. Streymoy, FAROE ISLANDS
40. Tórshavn, FAROE ISLANDS
41. Tórshavn, FAROE ISLANDS
42. Charlton Athletic FC, London, UK
43. Old Town Studio, Hastings, UK
44. Esplanade, St Leonards-on-Sea, UK
45. Glyne Gap Special Needs School, Bexton-on-Sea, UK
46. Cooden Beach, East Sussex, UK
47. North of Mexico City, MEXICO
48. North of Mexico City, MEXICO
49. Ihuatzio, MEXICO
50. Ihuatzio, MEXICO
51. Pátzcuaro, MEXICO
52. Tzintzuntzán, MEXICO
53. Pátzcuaro, MEXICO
54. Janutzio, MEXICO
55. Janutzio, MEXICO
56. Venice Beach, Los Angeles, USA
57. Venice Beach, Los Angeles, USA
58. Hollywood, Los Angeles, USA
59. Hollywood, Los Angeles, USA
60. Venice Beach, Los Angeles, USA
61. Venice Beach, Los Angeles, USA
62. St Leonards-on-Sea, East Sussex UK
63. Beckenham, Kent, UK
64. Chevening, Kent, UK
65. Cooden Beach, East Sussex, UK

In 2006 the film-maker drove around the entire coastline of Britain with his seven-year-old daughter, Eden, and his grandmother, Gladys. Like Kötting, Gladys is a strong and eccentric character. She is a woman who hates thunderstorms and mice, wears a tea cosy for a hat and dreams of being a lollypop lady. On the trio's coastal odyssey Gladys rows a boat out to at sea, camps under the stars and chats about grizzly suicide stories at Beachy Head with an uncomprehending German family. For both women in Kötting's journey, mortality was waiting in the shadows – Gladys was 87, Eden suffering from a potentially life-threatening genetic disorder.

It was a three-month journey designed to spend some time together 'before the opportunity was missed' (Kötting). The film-maker recorded the journey in *Gallivant* (1997), as the trio weaved their way along some 6,000 miles (9,650 km) of coast. Snapshots of British life on the coast are captured as we hear fishermen's songs, eavesdrop on teenagers in a Welsh village and the conversations of elderly folk at a bowls match.

'Do you think everyone is striving for recognition?' Kötting shouts, on a cold winter's day in Scotland, after throwing himself fully clothed into the sea. Halfway along, he fractures his leg and we join him in A&E. Kötting's cavalier approach to journeys and life itself ensures that injuries become a common theme in his travels.

That same year, Kötting's father died, inspiring an altogether stranger journey. He had a 12-foot (3.7-m) inflatable tombstone made, on to which was printed a picture of his father laughing, attired in a three-piece grey suit. The inflatable, which became known as the 'Deadad', accompanied Kötting – together with a generator and industrial electric fan – on a journey around the world in which he visited 65 places that had great significance to the two of them (Kötting's dad died at 65).

Kötting inflated the Deadad outside the house where he was conceived, by the church where his parents had been campanologists, in the street by his first office and the beach where Kötting lost his virginity. Kötting and his inflatable dad must have made for a bizarre sight. From Europe, Kötting travelled to Mexico for the Day of the Dead celebrations with his daughter Eden in tow, and then to America to visit family.

At each location, the towering Deadad was inflated, filmed, deflated, re-inflated and sometimes carried flapping out the window of a car. The Deadad was used as a trampoline in a family garden, taken surfing on the ocean, and in the USA joined everyone at a family dinner.

Halfway through his Deadad journey Kötting got a surprise letter, informing him that he had a long-lost half-uncle and cousins courtesy of an illicit dalliance of his grandfather's when he was stationed in the Faroe Islands during the Second World War. It prompted Kötting to make an inflatable 'Deadad's Deadad', and the pair were taken to these remote islands, halfway between Norway and Iceland, to the home where his long-lost uncle had been born.

FOR KÖTTING, the irreverent quality of travelling with an inflatable tomb bearing your father's image was not entirely driven by Dadaism. The journey was also a chance to 'mull over the rage [he] felt towards the dad'. An unpredictable and angry man, Kötting's father was prone to violent outbursts towards members of his family, once even pushing and locking his wife in a deep freezer. In travelling with Deadad, Kötting was finally able to have some control over his father, to celebrate some of his better qualities – his laughter – and have time to process a complex relationship that many of us have with the people who raised us. At the very end of his journey, Kötting climbed inside the Deadad, to go 'inside his very being'.

The gonzo journalist Hunter S. Thompson made it clear throughout much of his life that his death would come via his own hands, from one of his precious firearms. He finally took his own life in 2005 with a bullet through the head, having also left plans for his ashes to be fired 500 feet (150 m) into the air from a canon, and for the building of a giant monument of a fist clutching a peyote button – Thompson's self-created motif. Thanks to a friendship with Johnny Depp, the $2 million needed to secure Thompson's wish was found. After Thompson had been fired into the atmosphere, those paying tribute partied until dawn.

Unsurprisingly, Kötting's decidedly unconventional approach to life has also led him to question his own mortality and the final journeys of his body up to and after death. Unlike Thompson self-aggrandizing and costly send-off, Kötting's planned one feels more in keeping with the spirit of a true gonzo traveller and documentarian.

I have considered my suicide often – to swim into the Channel which I do all year round, to drift off and drown in its waters. I won't always be strong; I don't want life to linger on like for some people I've known and expect others to have responsibility for caring for me. I want to take control of my own demise. I want it to be heroic lite, a disintegration into the ocean.
Andrew Kötting (2018)

In the event of a natural death, however, the final journey of Kötting's mortal remains might be cost-free but they would cause a few logistical issues. *DB*

There's a big sacrificial stone in the middle of the forest in the Pyrenees, near where we have a house. I've sacrificed many animals there over the years. I leave them on this stone overnight and in the morning they're gone. I want to have my head left on the rock to see what spirit of the forest comes – wild boar, fox or wolverine perhaps – to take it on its final journey. Whatever's left, my lover Leila can chuck into the English Channel.
Andrew Kötting (2018)

Kötting with Deadad
(and Deadad's Deadad)

SEEKER'S DIRECTORY

Films

Swandown (dir. Andrew Kötting, 2012)
Iain Sinclair and Andrew Kotting take a surreal water journey in a swan-shaped pedalo from the seaside in Hastings to Hackney in London, via the English inland waterways and with the help of magician Alan Moore and comedian Stewart Lee.

Gallivant (dir. Andrew Kötting, 1997)
Kotting's finest hour; a playful and fascinating trip around the entire coast of Britain with his daughter and dynamic grandmother.

Book

In the Wake of a Deadad, Andrew Kötting (Kent Institute of Art & Design, 2006)
A scrapbook of photos, letters and maps from the film and exhibition of Kötting's travels with an inflatable tomb bearing his father's image.

Becalmed: tales of isolation at sea

Alain Bombard: the French doctor who survived at sea on saltwater, plankton and freshly squeezed fish | Donald Crowhurst: the 'weekend sailor' who travelled around the world without leaving the Atlantic

Bring to mind tales of nightmarish journeys under sail, and you might well imagine high seas, rogue waves, ships dashed on rocks – tales of human resilience pitted against an unrelenting and omnipotent ocean. But what of the times when the sea tires of tossing boats about like bath toys and renders them becalmed? Held hostage within a windless ocean, given leave even from the need to sail, captives can flounder in their thoughts for weeks, months, even years on end.

The next two journeys play out in one of the strangest places in the world. A shoreless oval of water in the North Atlantic measuring some 2,000 by 700 miles (3,200 by 1,125 km), the mysterious Sargasso Sea is renowned for its disquieting calms. Bounded by ocean currents on all sides, the windless sea slowly revolves like the eye of a hurricane. It is an altogether singular place: desolate above water but teeming with peculiar creatures below. A knotted mass of free-floating sargassum seaweed covers the surface, picked over by crabs, shrimp and curious fish; most of the world's freshwater eels are spawned here. Tales of ghost ships abound, their skeleton crews left to starve or go insane while their sails hung listlessly.

Into this eerie, mid-Atlantic pond sailed two men, 16 years apart; both were determined to prove a point. The first was a French doctor who believed it possible to cross the Atlantic relying solely on the sea for sustenance. He had set out from the Canaries in a tiny inflatable lifeboat 40 days earlier, and by the time he neared the Sargasso Sea, he was categorically lost. The second was a 'weekend sailor' from Somerset who had mistakenly signed up to a solo round-the-world yacht race. An

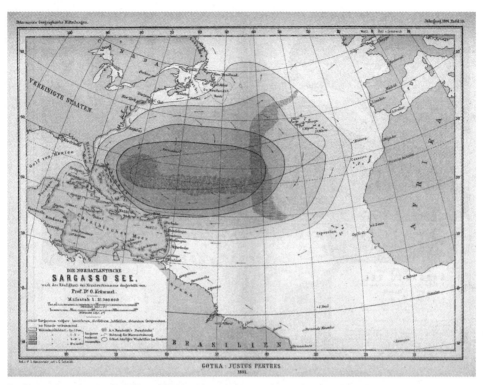

The Sargasso Sea, a gigantic eddy 5000 miles (8050 km) in circumference and covered in a great knotted mass of seaweed, has always been a navigational hazard for sailors.

inventor of navigational gadgets, this man knew precisely where he was, but he was desperately out of his depth.

Alain Bombard 1924–2005

In the spring of 1951 French doctor Alain Bombard was asleep in the residents' quarters of a hospital in Boulogne-sur-mer when he was woken by a call: the trawler *Notre-Dame-de-Peyragues* had missed her course in the mist and broken up on the outer breakwater of the harbour. Bombard arrived at a scene that would stay with him for the rest of his life: 43 men piled up on top of each other 'like dislocated puppets', their feet bare and lifejackets intact. The doctor and his colleagues failed to revive a single one of them.

Bombard thought about how one simple error of navigation had caused the deaths of 43 men and orphaned 78 children. He thought of the 150 fishermen killed each year just in his region of France, and the 200,000 men, women and children who

According to *Time* magazine, Alain Bombard became interested in survival techniques in 1951 after being rescued from an unsuccessful attempt to swim the English Channel. Over the course of five days, he and a friend had survived on just half a kilogram of butter.

suffered the same fate every year around the world. More than a quarter of them made it to a lifeboat, only to die in prolonged agony from lack of food and water, or the well-documented perils of losing one's mind at sea.

Bombard became convinced that castaways could survive for long periods of time by feasting on what the sea could provide, and that countless lives could be saved if lifeboats were fitted with a few simple pieces of equipment: fish hooks, fine nets for collecting plankton – a source of vitamin C – and presses for squeezing fresh water out of fish. He even argued that drinking small amounts of seawater – a maximum of one and a half pints (almost 1 litre) per day – could prolong life, contradicting centuries of evidence to the contrary. But how could he prove such a thing?

TO DEMONSTRATE HIS point, in 1952, Bombard embarked on a singular voyage. In the hope of saving thousands of future castaways from madness and death, the French doctor determined to sail across the Atlantic Ocean in a 15-foot (4.5-m) inflatable dinghy, using only the sea for sustenance. Onboard the aptly named *L'Hérétique,* he would have a sextant and a watch for navigating, his fishing kit, and a tarpaulin for shelter and catching rainwater. Emergency rations would be sealed within the craft, and checked by officials once he reached the other side of the Atlantic.

Bombard set his sights on the West Indies, plotting a course between two dreaded dangers: the Doldrums and the Sargasso Sea. The former was an area of low pressure, where two powerful trade winds 'meet in a tremendous conflict in a no-man's land of violent storms, unpredictable turbulence and disquieting calms' (Alain Bombard, *The Bombard Story,* 1953). The latter was far more frightening.

On 19 October 1952 Bombard set off from the Canaries, cheered on by friends and accompanied by a 'veritable convoy' of yachts; all the ships in port sounded their sirens. A three-masted schooner, a training ship for the Spanish navy, dipped her sails as he left the harbour by way of a salute, and Bombard saw this as a good omen: this survivor of the days of sail was a reminder of the millions of lives 'engulfed in the man-eating sea', and his experimental voyage would bring new hope and salvation for future generations.

Even though the stiff breeze that sped him away from the harbour abandoned his lifeboat shortly after and left him drifting, he slept well that first night, tucking his tarpaulin up to his neck like a blanket and dropping off under a 'lovely, luminous sky'. It didn't take long for the reality of his solo voyage to sink in, however. After two more nights drifting aimlessly, a breeze picked up and pushed him further into the Atlantic. The zephyr soon became a tempest, which tossed the *Hérétique* about like a cork. Confident in the lifeboat's stability, Bombard decided to sleep it out, waking soon after to find himself completely surrounded by water: a wave had broken over him.

He began frantically bailing, scooping water out with his hat for the next two hours while more waves broke over the dingy. Being only a few days into his voyage, however, Bombard was still pumped up on optimism and a sense of purpose. He felt confident in his ability to weather the storms. 'I can only say to my fellow castaways: be more obstinate than the sea, and you will win' (*The Bombard Story*).

As October wore on, the *Hérétique* continued to be buffeted by gales. The sail ripped; if he managed to sleep at all, Bombard did so shivering, encrusted with salt. When not bailing water or stitching up his sail, he mused on the nature of fear and despair. Above all, he was afraid of fear itself, recognising that increasingly tiredness and exhaustion led him to expect the worst, which in turn made him 'weak and cowardly' (*The Bombard Story*).

Bombard recognized a paradox in the level of his morale. When things were going badly, he managed to cope with it, but once there was some slight improvement, he began to fear the worst. To keep his growing melancholia at bay, he busied himself with catching fish. He squeezed water out of the small ones using a makeshift press and cut slits in the larger ones, drinking straight from their bodies like some Gollum of the Atlantic. He trapped seabirds and ate them raw and netted two daily spoonfuls of plankton to top up his vitamin C levels and keep scurvy at bay.

COME LATE OCTOBER, Bombard had become fixated by the condition of his boat. Each day, he inspected the inflatable craft meticulously, noting where friction had worn the rubberized canvas thin, prising barnacles off to keep its undercarriage in tip-top condition, and putting his ear to the material to check for sounds of rubbing like a doctor with a stethoscope.

Imagine his horror when, in the middle of the Atlantic, he began to be hounded by swordfish. By now, Bombard had become a dab hand at batting away sharks, but he was defenceless against swordfish, fearing that he would enrage them if he engaged in conflict (swordfish were, he had read, prone to fits of fury). He described '12 hours of terror' fending off 'a large swordfish of undeniably menacing aspect … seemingly in a rage, his dorsal fin raised like hackles' (*The Bombard Story*).

It's worth noting that, by this point, Bombard was also completely lost. '[I] can no longer determine my longitude with certainty,' he admitted on 26 October. 'I shall just have to guess it from the time the sun reaches the meridian' (*The Bombard Story*). Stubbornly, he pushed on, but his body was beginning to show the effects of his journey. He started to lose toe nails and developed a rash. Losing weight, he found it impossible to get comfortable; every position he sat or lay in caused him pain.

By November, having failed to read an accurate longitude for weeks, Bombard was convinced that he was approaching the end of his journey, unaware that he hadn't yet passed the Cape Verde Islands. Expecting to see land each new day, and being sorely disappointed, his mood started to dwindle.

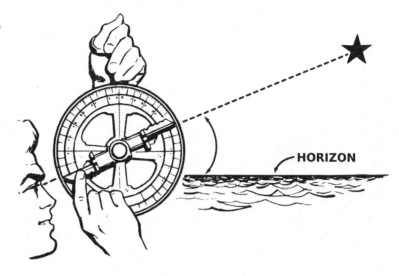

A sextant is a navigation instrument that measures the angular distance between two visible objects, such as the sun at noon or Polaris at night, and the horizon.

HORIZON

I thought that solitude was something I would be able to master... I had been too presumptuous... It was a vast presence which engulfed me. Its spell could not be broken, any more than the horizon could be brought nearer.
Bombard, The Bombard Story

As the days wore on, with still no sign of land, Bombard became increasingly superstitious: Wednesdays took on a special meaning; the number of damp matches he struck before one lit became the number of days remaining; he believed that he could calculate wind speed by simply listening to its note against the sail.

Bombard also became obsessed with seabirds, which teased him to despair with their promise of land. He developed a persecution mania and became incensed with rage at his 'raft book' (a manual for castaways), which promised that certain species could only be seen within a hundred miles (160 km) of land. The only tangible presence being his own, Bombard began to take comfort in the creatures around him, documenting his encounters with all the drama and character you would expect from someone who hadn't had human contact for months.

He was visited at four o'clock each day by the same petrel and was kept company for almost the entire journey by a shoal of 'dolphins' – actually dorados, a large type of fish, which jostled around his boat. 'I was to get to know their spiny backs well, recognising them as old friends,' he wrote. '... I was always struck by the beauty of these creatures, swimming parallel to me, and leaving phosphorescent wakes like some shooting star.' His life began to resemble that of the creatures around him. 'I began to share their sensations and reactions,' he wrote, 'eating the same food and catching the same flying fish.'

ALAIN BOMBARD'S JOURNEY ACROSS THE ATLANTIC

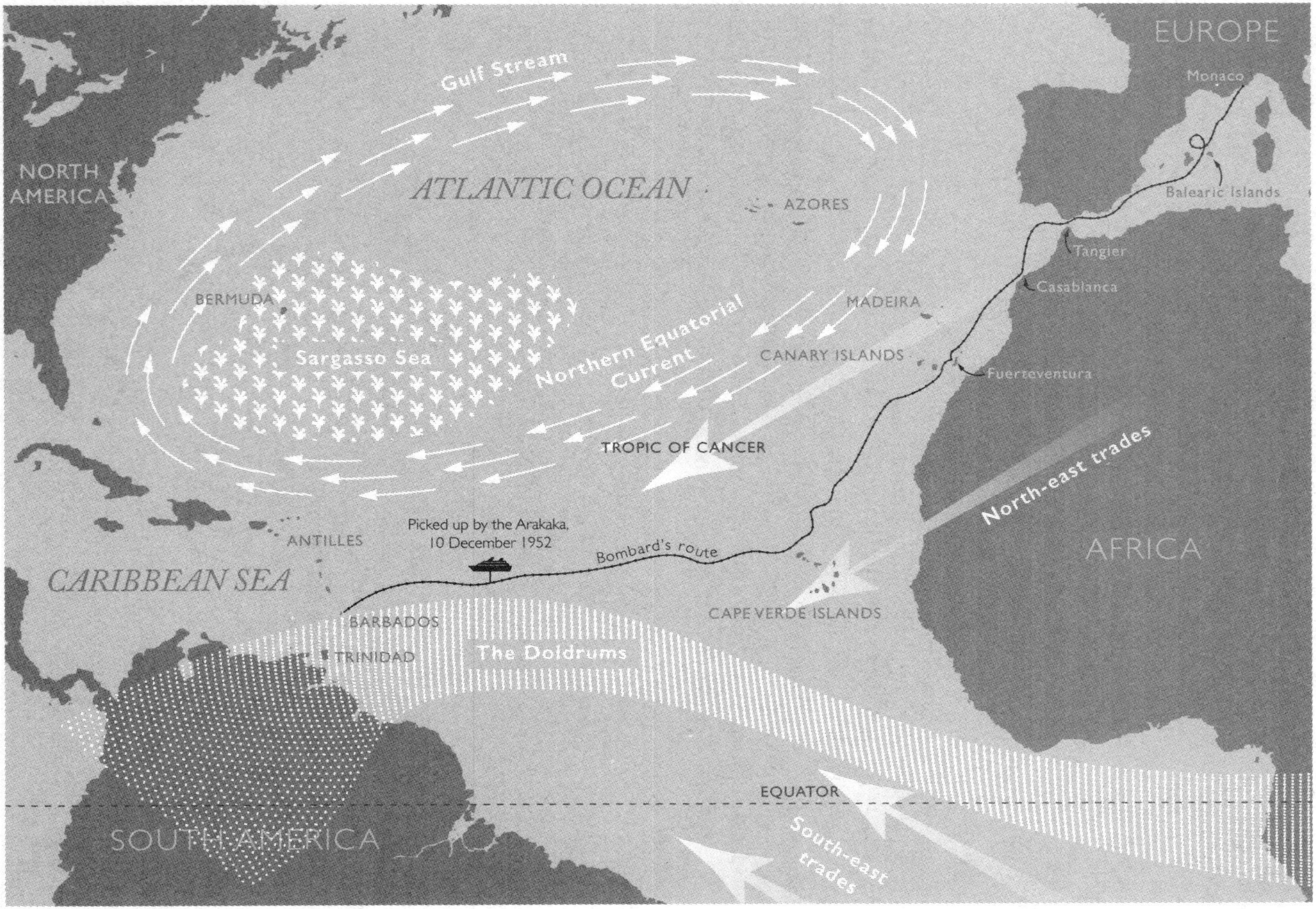
EUROPE
Monaco
Balearic Islands
Tangier
Casablanca
Fuerteventura
NORTH AMERICA
Gulf Stream
ATLANTIC OCEAN
AZORES
MADEIRA
CANARY ISLANDS
BERMUDA
Sargasso Sea
Northern Equatorial Current
TROPIC OF CANCER
North-east trades
AFRICA
ANTILLES
Picked up by the Arakaka, 10 December 1952
Bombard's route
CARIBBEAN SEA
BARBADOS
TRINIDAD
CAPE VERDE ISLANDS
The Doldrums
EQUATOR
SOUTH AMERICA
South-east trades

Some encounters were less welcome than others. His inflatable boat was attacked by sharks on multiple occasions, the giant predators flipping on to their backs as they passed below, flashing their teeth. He reassured himself with a brief glint of his former optimism: 'I comforted myself with the thought of how difficult it must be to bite a football.'

In between the horror of shark attacks and the creeping onset of paranoia, Bombard experienced moments of pure wonder – a half-eaten shearwater carcass illuminating the sail with a ghostly phosphorescence – and felt loneliness unlike anything he had experienced. At times, he became overwhelmed by the beauty of his surroundings, writing long eloquent odes to the ocean. Staying awake one evening to check the time of the moonrise, Bombard was overcome by the feeling of what a strange and formidable element the sea is, writing:

> It seems to form part of a system so entirely different from normal existence that it might belong to another planet. But there it is at my feet, alive yet inscrutable. Here and there lights appear in the depths... They look like stars half hidden in a cloudy night sky. The fish around me leap and swim to and fro, protagonists of an unseen and mysterious existence. Life at the surface is only the thin upper layer of another world.
> *Journal entry from Bombard,* The Bombard Story

AROUND MID-NOVEMBER, time began to weigh heavily on Bombard. He suffered a 14-day bout of diarrhoea and was struggling to sleep. 'Forty-eight hours without sleep, and I am utterly depressed; the ordeal is really beginning to get me down,' he wrote on 11 November. 'It really seemed as if the sea was in mourning.' To top it off, the skin on his feet had started to peel away in great strips and he was down to his last couple of toenails.

PRINCIPAL CONSTITUENTS OF FISH
Percentages by weight

Fish	Water %	Proteins %	Fats %
Ray	76.80–82.20	18.20–24.20	0.10–1.60
Basking shark	68.00	15.20	16.00
Dorado	77.00–78.89	17.25–19.00	1.00–3.31
Sardine	78.34	16.30–21.0	2.00–12.00
Anchovy	76.19	21.92	1.11
Bass	77.00–79.94	18.53–19.96	0.84–2.50
Mackerel	68.84–74.27	17.59–23.10	5.14–8.36
Tuna	58.50	27.00	13.00

(credit: The Bombard Story)

Towards the end of November, the wind disappeared entirely and Bombard drifted for over a week. Unbeknown to him, he had reached the edge of the Sargasso Sea. His mood was ebbing and his eyes ached from straining on the horizon. 'I have had enough,' he wrote, underlining it in his log. 'Forty days is enough for any man.'

By December, he admitted to being 'prey to every emotion', stewing in his own thoughts under a terrible sun. He tried to calculate how long it would take him to reach land, moving at his current pace of about 100 yards (90 m) per hour. 'I shall be dead first, either burnt to a crisp, or a victim of thirst and hunger,' he wrote gloomily. 'Everything seems to conspire against me.'

Bombard's paranoia became overwhelming; he believed the clouds were deliberately avoiding the sun so as to deny him shade. He decided that he would not attempt to fight the next storm, trusting his fate to God. 'What have I done to deserve all this?' he wrote, dictating his will and final wishes, and holding the authors of his castaways' handbook accountable for his inevitable death.

JUST WHEN Bombard fell into despair, a miracle happened – and it did, in fact, fall on a Wednesday. He ran into the *Arakaka*, a passenger cargo steamer out of Liverpool. Shouting over the tannoy, they confirmed his location – and it was 600 miles (966 km) further from the West Indies than he had calculated. The news hit Bombard like a hammer. 'This is it,' he shouted, 'fifty-three days, I give up.' And he scrambled aboard.

He accepted a shower and a light meal – a fried egg, spoonful of cabbage and a slither of liver. In hindsight, this was a bad move on all accounts. Not only would he be held to account for it on his return – eating this meal had invalidated the terms of his experiment – the sudden return to a normal diet nearly killed him over the following days. But his need for human contact (rather than food) was too great and accepting this hospitality, arguably, saved his life.

The encounter gave Bombard the morale boost he so sorely needed, and he set off with renewed vigour on 10 December, having been taught how to read longitude. On Christmas Eve 1952, the French doctor staggered on to a Barbados beach, 65 days after setting out from the Canaries. He had lost 55 pounds (25 kg) in weight, was severely anaemic, and found it hard to walk, but he was alive. And, crucially, he had proved his point, at least in his own mind.

In the midst of his despair, Alain Bombard had been offered human contact. He embraced it, scrabbling to get onboard the *Arakaka*, even though the move would mean the failure of his experiment in the minds of his many critics. The protagonist of our next tale of isolation at sea, however, was so bound up in his own self-constructed reality, he found it impossible to make this potentially life-saving act.

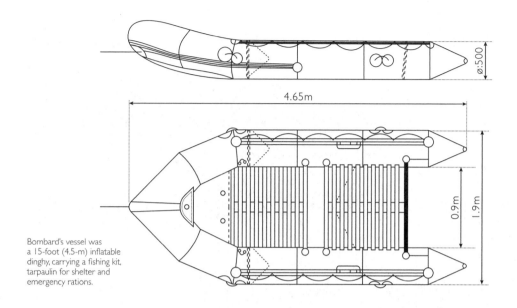

4.65m

ø:500

0.9m

1.9m

Bombard's vessel was a 15-foot (4.5-m) inflatable dinghy, carrying a fishing kit, tarpaulin for shelter and emergency rations.

Donald Crowhurst 1932–1969

Donald Crowhurst was an orphan of the British Empire, born in India under the British Raj in 1932. His father was a superintendent with the North Western Railway Company but, after independence in 1947, the family were forced to move back to England to meagre savings and reduced circumstances. Crowhurst's mother was highly strung, superior and anxious about their fall in status; his father ended up a porter in a jam factory and, not long after arriving back in England, died of a heart attack while gardening. With his family falling on hard times, Crowhurst was forced to forego his promised Cambridge University education and train instead as an apprentice. He excelled in electronic engineering, but then drifted from job to job, ever aware of his potential to achieve great things.

In the mid-1960s, Crowhurst was doing rather well for himself – living with his wife, Clare, and their four children in a large rambling home near Bridgwater, Somerset. A compulsive tinkerer with a knack for dreaming up gadgets and coming up with daring solutions, he was on the verge of a successful career in electronics. He had invented a radio location device for sailing, which he called the Navicator, and had built up a small company, Electron Utilisation Ltd, around its success.

Crowhurst was an intelligent and talented man: popular, charming and headstrong.

Donald Crowhurst poses on the
deck of *Teignmouth Electron.*

He saw himself as the hero in his own life; and life itself as game, to be played out against authority and society. He was also persuasive and fond of tasking risks, and friends would often get swept away by his schemes. 'The thing about Donald was that he thought of himself as God,' said another friend, Peter Beard. 'Everything in his life revolved around his belief in himself, and he was always so quick and clever he could make others believe in him too.'

In the late 1960s, however, Crowhurst's business took a tumble. His main investor, local millionaire Stanley Best, decided to pull funding. And yet somehow Crowhurst managed to turn the situation around and convince Best to pump his money, instead, into backing him on a non-stop, round-the-world sailing race being launched by *The Sunday Times*.

> He seemed to have this capacity to convince himself that everything was going to be wonderful, and hopeless situations were only temporary setbacks. This enthusiasm, I admit, was infectious. But, as I now realise, it was the product of that kind of over-imaginative mind that was always dreaming reality into the state it wanted it to be.
> *Stanley Best, quoted in Nicholas Tomalin and Ron Hall,* The Strange Last Journey of Donald Crowhurst, *1970*

Circumnavigating the world wasn't the first maritime project Crowhurst had got excited about. He had thought of reenacting Thor Heyerdahl's *Kon-Tiki* expedition, in which the Norwegian floated 5,000 miles (8,050 km) across the Pacific on a hand-made raft. And he also fancied having a go at recreating Alain Bombard's solo voyage across the Atlantic in a lifeboat, existing solely on raw fish and plankton.

The Sunday Times Golden Globe Race, however, had the potential to kick-start his business and skyrocket his status. Up for grabs were two prizes: a 'golden globe' for the first person to complete the race, and a £5,000 cash prize for the sailor who circumnavigated the world in the quickest time. More tempting than either of these, however, was the potential for publicity. Crowhurst's yacht would be fitted with all his latest navigational gadgets and inventions – winning the race would show the world what he was capable of.

The small print of his agreement with Stanley Best, however, raised the stakes to an inordinate level. Best would underwrite the costs of a custom-built trimaran – a racing yacht with two floats on either side of the main hull – but, if the voyage failed, Crowhurst would be forced to buy the boat back, at a price that would effectively close his business and cost him his home. With typical zeal, Crowhurst leapt at these potentially life-ruining odds, and started making arrangements.

COMPETING IN A non-stop, round-the-world race was a lonely prospect, requiring level-headedness and unshakeable practicability. Participants would be looking at around eight months at sea, battling terrifying conditions, fixing their boats en route and never stepping foot on land. Crowhurst's eight rivals included veteran sailors, transatlantic oarsmen, former naval officers and an ex-merchant seaman. Thirty-six-year-old Crowhurst, on the other hand, was a 'weekend sailor' with something to prove to the world.

To help craft his story as the underdog – Britain's brave boy – Crowhurst hired publicist Rodney Hallworth, a former crime reporter for the *Daily Mail*, a larger-than-life hack who could down pints of bitter without missing a single quote (*The Strange Last Journey*). Over the months that followed, Hallworth would become a dab hand at translating Crowhurst's vague cabled words into effervescent prose and feeding it to the press.

Things didn't get off to the best start. The building of Crowhurst's trimaran, *Teignmouth Electron*, had been chaotic and fraught with drama, leaving him with a 35-foot (10.7-m) boat that leaked. On the last date he could have entered the race, Crowhurst was under prepared and underfunded, frantically packing the boat on the quay.

Sensing a catastrophe, BBC film-maker Donald Kerr quietly told his crew to switch the tone of the coverage; they were no longer promoting an underdog triumph but witnessing the unfolding of a tragedy. On the eve of the launch, Kerr actually called off filming and instructed his team to chip in, scattering them about the town to procure lifejackets and emergency flares. Crowhurst, by this point, was shaking from lack of sleep and food, and kept muttering 'It's no good, it's no good' under his breath.

In hindsight, it was clear the electronic engineer did not want to go, but by this point the stakes were too high. Plus, this was Donald Crowhurst: the invincible. If he set his mind to something, then he was convinced that he would succeed at it.

The night before leaving, Crowhurst let his guard down just enough to admit to his wife: 'Darling, I'm very disappointed in the boat. She's not right. I'm not prepared. If I leave with things in this hopeless state, will you go out of your mind with worry?' Swallowing her own reservations, Claire replied: 'If you give up now, will you be unhappy for the rest of your life?' Donald Crowhurst didn't answer; he cried until morning.

ON 31 OCTOBER 1968, Donald Crowhurst set out from Teignmouth harbour. His boat was still without masts or rigging, and the steering gear was dodgy. Even as he tacked down the English Channel, screws unwound themselves – and he hadn't packed many spares. 'Can't keep cannibalising from other spots forever!' he wrote in his logbook. 'The thing will soon fall to bits!'

Crowhurst spent the first day tidying up the coils of colour-coded wires that wound around the bulkheads and across the cabin roof. The wires ended in a fray of loose ends beside a space where his computer should have been – Crowhurst's revolutionary control system, which would enable him to remotely maintain his boat and push it

A replica of *Teignmouth Electron*, used for shooting a film about Crowhurst's voyage.

to extraordinary speeds, had not been finished in time. He tidied up batteries, tools and rolls of film into Tupperware containers; he cut his finger trying to hoist a radar detector, and soon became seasick.

As he made slow progress down the Brittany coast, Crowhurst comforted himself with the conviction that he was embarking on a most extraordinary journey. 'I feel like somebody who's been given a tremendous opportunity to impart a message, some profound observation that will save the world,' he recorded on tape for the BBC.

Two weeks later, the cockpit hatch sprung a leak and flooded his engine and electrics. Not only had he risked his home, his business and his reputation on a faulty boat that was unlikely to survive the Southern Oceans, Crowhurst was now struck with the possibility of having to continue without electricity and radio contact.

15 November: Racked by the growing awareness that I must soon decide whether or not I can go on in the face of the actual situation. What a bloody awful decision – to chuck it in at this stage – what a bloody awful decision!
Tomalin and Hall, The Strange Last Voyage

Listing his difficulties in the logbook, Crowhurst thrashed out what to do, pondering over the nature of failure and desperately trying to salvage something from the situation. He concluded that it was impossible to make a decision at this point, and pushed on.

On 10 December, Crowhurst reported a record-breaking speed of 243 miles (391 km) in a day, which his publicist enthusiastically passed on to *The Sunday Times*. Crowhurst was back in the game. In truth, the lone sailor had been listlessly circling just north of Madeira; detailed sketches he'd made of Funchal harbour suggest he was deliberating whether to make for port, before changing his mind.

In the run-up to this press announcement, Crowhurst had clearly weighed up his two options (returning a failure or risking death) and come up with a third course of action. He had ceased confiding in his logbook – the daily record of a sailor's location and ordeals – and, instead, had been meticulously taking down celestial sights, almost like he was practising his navigational skills. Then, on 6 December, Crowhurst opened a second notebook. In this new 'logbook two', he plotted his real navigational progress. In 'logbook one', he began a new narrative – a meticulous trail of fabricated positions, which pushed *Teignmouth Electron* further into the Atlantic, on course to sail around the world. The deception had begun.

Crowhurst set out from Teignmouth harbour on 31 October 1968, sailing a boat without masts or rigging, and with a dodgy steering gear.

PLOTTING ONE'S FRAUDULENT journey around the world is much harder than you might already imagine – arguably requiring greater mathematical skill than navigating the actual course. It involves recording faraway weather forecasts, imagining geography and long hours of mathematical calculations – and you have to show your workings. A gifted sums-man, Crowhurst was up to the challenge, detailing his false locations with neat and fastidious notes; he added margin notes on the weather and meals he'd cooked, too, for good measure.

He also began feeding false stories to his publicist, who exaggerated the drama further: a run-of-the-mill rainstorm became a 45-knot squall that shattered his wind vane. On 20 December, Crowhurst reported travelling 170 miles (274 km) in a day and nearing the Brazilian coast. He had, in fact, travelled 13 miles (21 km) that day. He was stuck in the Doldrums: a belt of low pressure, thundery weather and fluky winds around the equator where ships can drift for weeks. Only a handful of detractors, most notably pioneering sailor Sir Francis Chichester, doubted his luck at passing through the Doldrums unscathed.

COME CHRISTMAS, Crowhurst's mood took a turn for the worse. 'There is something rather melancholy and desperate about this part of the Atlantic Ocean,' he recorded. 'Not that I'm depressed or feeling sorry for myself by any means, but … Christmas … does tend to make one a little melancholy.'

He had a strained call with Clare, who hid her own struggles and desperate financial concerns just as well as Crowhurst hid his. After the call, he sought out shortwave radio transmissions, grasping for human voices, and wrote gloomy poems. He dithered within 20 miles (32 km) of the Brazilian coast, perhaps close enough to see lights shimmering on the shore, then set out south-east, back to the Atlantic.

During this time Crowhurst was still feeding vague but outlandish bulletins to the press. By mid-January, he was 'well into the Indian Ocean'. His estimated arrival date back in the UK crept ever forward. To make matters even more stressful, Hallworth was misinterpreting Crowhurst's Morse code messages and, by 19 January, misconstrued one so spectacularly that he placed *Teignmouth Electron* some 4,000 miles (6,440 km) away from his true position. It was getting increasingly hard to keep up the ruse. Crowhurst was having to cross-reference and transcribe up to three different weather reports to make his phoney locations believable. It was all getting a bit much. Crowhurst sent a cable to say that he was sealing the cockpit hatch over his generator, and dropped out of contact for 11 weeks.

Meanwhile, *Teignmouth Electron* was still falling ever-so-steadily apart; the plywood was splitting and the hull leaking. This was no longer a craft that would survive the high seas of the Southern Ocean. An unseaworthy boat would have been a justifiable reason to give up. However, Hallworth's tall tales had by now placed Crowhurst too far away for him to land while keeping up the pretence. His closest port, according to the false course, was Madagascar; and he was still zig-zagging off the coast of Brazil. To give up now meant total downfall.

After further dithering, Crowhurst took a pit-stop in Río Salado in Brazil, disqualifying himself in the 'non-stop' competition but getting away with it when the coastguard disregarded his first name – taking it to be like the Spanish don (Mr) – and knocking his surname off, too. 'Charles Alfred' borrowed materials and patched up *Teignmouth Electron* as best he could then ate with the coastguard's family, although, with no common language, it was a silent affair.

CROWHURST'S GRAND PLAN was to reappear in the Atlantic (having never left it) around mid-April, break his radio silence, and rejoin the race for the final sprint home. First, he would detour to the Falkland Islands – to send a cable on a frequency used by a New Zealand radio station and give the impression that he was in the Pacific – and then he'd capture footage of stormy seas to vouch for his passage around Cape Horn. After leaving these last pieces of evidence, he would race home as fast as he could and, with luck, sneak in just after the current runner-up, Nigel Tetley. Coming third would mean he could save face and gain maximum publicity while avoiding having his logbooks scrutinized by the judges.

Remarkably, on the return leg, Crowhurst came close to matching some of his fabricated speeds – recording two genuine 200-mile (320-km) plus days on 4 and 5 May. However, his refound enthusiasm for 'sailorising' (as he called it) wasn't to last. On 23 May, Crowhurst heard the news that Tetley's boat *Victress* had been taken out by force 9 gales around the Azores. Forced on by the knowledge that Crowhurst was fast on his heels, his competitor had overstretched his boat. After eight months of lone sailing, Tetley was out of the race with only 1,100 miles (1,770 km) to go.

Crowhurst was now on to win the £5,000 cash prize. He would return a hero, share tales with genuine round-the-world sailors and have his logbooks examined by navigational savants. It was one thing to dupe a gullible and geographically impaired publicist, it was quite another to hold one's own around a table with navigations of the Southern Oceans.

The full force of this realization must have hit Crowhurst hard. After his initial burst of speed, he began, once more, to zigzag and drift. To make matters worse, Crowhurst's transmitter – his only way now of making human contact – was playing up. He spent the next two weeks soldering electronic components, stripping naked in the equatorial heat and working for 16 hours per day in his suffocating 8 by 9-feet (2.4 x 2.7-m) cabin surrounded by disemboweled radios and half-eaten tins of food.

On 22 June Crowhurst got the 'damn thing' working and fired off messages home. He was bombarded with replies. The BBC were arranging for a helicopter to meet him off-shore; 100,000 people were expected to cheer him into Teignmouth; Hallworth was working on the syndication rights for his future books. The pressure had reached boiling point. On 24 June, Donald Crowhurst turned off the transmitter, thumbed over a new page in 'logbook two' and wrote the title 'PHILOSOPHY'.

CROWHURST HADN'T brought any novels with him, choosing instead technical reads and Albert Einstein's *Relativity, the Special and General Theory*. Within its pages, the lone sailor found a new weight of meaning. He became obsessed with a paragraph in which Einstein states that, when faced with a mathematical impasse, he could exert his free will to make it disappear. Crowhurst took this to mean that the physicist, possessing a superior mind, was capable of using the power of his free will to exert a godlike control over the universe.

Crowhurst began feverishly writing – and didn't stop for the next 30 hours. As Teignmouth Electron drifted into the eerie, weed-choked waters of the Sargasso Sea, Crowhurst wrote 25,000 words in dense, scrawling handwriting, barely noticing his pencils blunting in his urgency to impart his life's great message.

> *if* creative abstraction is to act as a vehicle for the new entity, and to leave its hitherto stable state it lies within the power of creative abstraction to produce the phenomenon!!!!!!!!!!!!!!! We can bring it about by creative abstraction!
>
> Now we must be very careful about getting the answer right. We are at the point where our powers of abstraction are powerful enough to do tremendous damage… Like nuclear chain reactions in the matter system, our whole system of creative abstraction can be brought to the point of 'take off'… By writing these words I do signal the process to begin.
> *Tomalin and Hall*, The Strange Last Voyage

He had fallen upon the visionary understanding that he wanted to impact on the world. It was a 'profound realization' that a person of superior intelligence could, through sheer act of will, break free from the constraints of his physical existence. Crowhurst had found an escape from his impossible predicament, one founded in his own brilliance; he had worked out how to become divine.

Remarkably, in the midst of this feverish breakdown, a genuine opportunity for salvation arrived. A Norwegian cargo vessel called the *Cuyahoga* spotted the trimaran at 5pm on 25 June and came over to check if everything was OK. Starved of human contact and going out of his mind, this would have been just the time for Crowhurst to reach out. Instead, Crowhurst waved cheerfully to show that he didn't require assistance

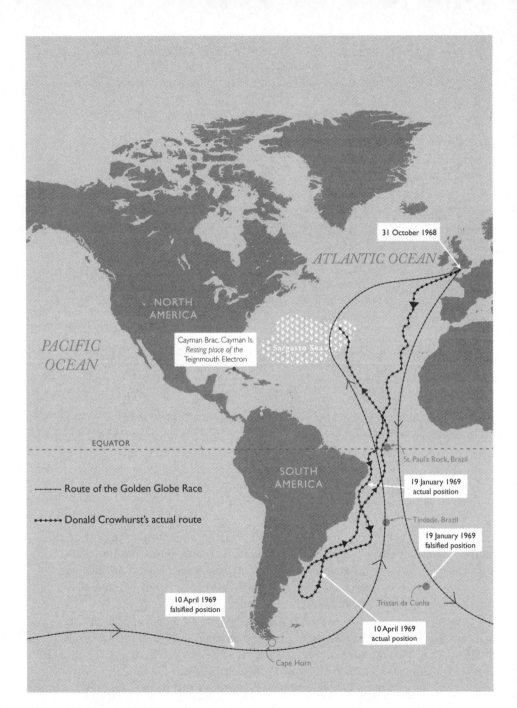

31 October 1968

ATLANTIC OCEAN

NORTH
AMERICA

PACIFIC
OCEAN

Cayman Brac, Cayman Is.
Resting place of the
Teignmouth Electron

Sargasso Sea

EQUATOR

St. Paul's Rock, Brazil

—— Route of the Golden Globe Race

•••••• Donald Crowhurst's actual route

SOUTH
AMERICA

19 January 1969
actual position

Tindade, Brazil

19 January 1969
falsified position

10 April 1969
falsified position

Tristan da Cunha

10 April 1969
actual position

Cape Horn

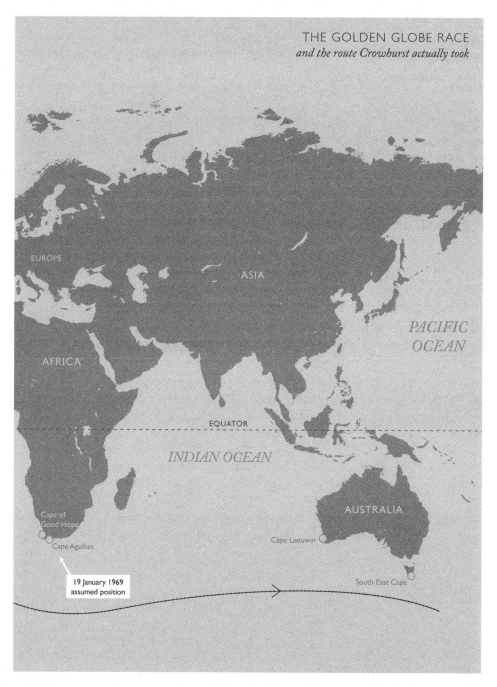

THE GOLDEN GLOBE RACE
and the route Crowhurst actually took

EUROPE

ASIA

PACIFIC OCEAN

AFRICA

EQUATOR

INDIAN OCEAN

Cape of
Good Hope

Cape Agulhas

Cape Leeuwin

AUSTRALIA

19 January 1969
assumed position

South East Cape

On 10 April 1969, Crowhurst broke radio silence, claiming to have cleared Cape Horn (*left*) and be heading home: 'What's new ocean-bashingwise?' he asked, cheerfully.

In the dead calm of the Sargasso Sea, clumps of Sargassum weed can stretch for miles along the surface.

and let the *Cuyahoga* sail on by. He then returned to his cabin to pen a history of the past 2,000 years, exploring how exceptional men had used their brilliance to shock the world into change. As he became even more entangled in his own mind, the strands of Sargassum seaweed knotted ever more tightly around his yacht.

WHEN CROWHURST EMERGED on to the deck over a week later, his wristwatch had wound down and he had no idea what time or day it was. He spent a while trying to work it out, using his nautical almanac, and concluded that it was 10am on 1 July. His notes from this point on are annotated by the precise minutes and seconds, as he perceived them. At '10 29', he wrote what could be seen as a confession:

10 29
...Now is revealed the true
nature and purpose and power
of the game offence I am

I am what I am and I
see the nature of my offence

He then addressed an appeal – to God or the devil who has been making up the rules to this terrible game he has been playing – to play it fairly next time.

I will only resign this game
if you agree that
the next occasion that this
game is played it will be played
according to the rules that are devised by
my great god who has
revealed at last to his son
not only the exact nature
of the reason for games but
has also revealed the truth of
the way of the ending of the
next game that
It is finished –
It is finished
IT IS THE MERCY

His entry concludes with a countdown, ending precisely at 11.20am and 40 seconds.

11 17 00
It is the time for your
move to begin

I have not need to prolong
the game

It has been a good game that
must be ended at the
I will play this game when
I choose I will resign the
game 11 20 40 There is
no reason for harmful

Crowhurst had reached the end of his logbook; his time had run out.

On 10 July the *Teignmouth Electron* was discovered ghosting in the middle of the Atlantic with only its mizzen sail raised. The captain of the Royal Mail ship *Picardy*

A replica of Donald Crowhurst's boat *Teignmouth Electron*, shot in Bristol harbour with a film crew aboard.

The wreck of the *Teignmouth Electron* is slowly disintegrating on a beach in the Cayman Islands.

stepped aboard. Inside the cabin, dishes were piled up in the sink, a sweat-soaked sleeping bag lay rumpled on the bunk, radios and transmitters spilled out their copper wires, a soldering iron was poised on an empty milk tin. Laid out on the table were three logbooks: one real, one false and one documenting his radio contact with the world.

That evening, two local policeman arrived at Crowhurst's home and told his wife: 'The boat's been found, and he's not on it.' The general consensus is that, at 11.20am and 40 seconds, Donald Crowhurst jumped into the Sargasso Sea.

IT'S WELL DOCUMENTED that long periods at sea can impair mental function. The singular combination of sleep deprivation, malnourishment, extreme fatigue and sensory deprivation can cause hallucinations and delusions. (*Off the Deep End: A History of Madness at Sea*, Nic Compton, Bloomsbury, 2017). When Bombard and Crowhurst were actively sailing, their minds were occupied. When left adrift, however, they were free to wallow in their own thoughts. Each began suffering from paranoia – a psychotic episode in which deluded ideas acquire a complex and intricate structure, held together by strong internal logic. Bombard's was built on a system of persecution; Crowhurst's constructed on delusions of grandeur.

But beyond the usual story of despair at sea, these two stories reveal what happens when into this already-heady concoction you add the element of winning or losing. Both men had manoeuvred themselves into a situation where they were not just pitted against the ocean, but also against themselves. The difference was that, when offered a chance of salvation, Alain Bombard was willing to risk losing the game he had chosen to play; Donald Crowhurst, sadly, wasn't. *JT*

SEEKER'S DIRECTORY

Books
The Bombard Story, Dr Alain Bombard (Andre Deutsch, 1953)
Bombard's complete account of his journey first across the Meditarrean Sea and then the Atlantic Ocean in a 15-foot (4.5-m) inflatable dinghy called *L'Hérétique*, using only the sea for sustenance.

Off the Deep End: A History of Madness at Sea, Nic Compton (Bloomsbury, 2017)
A fascinating book that explores the sea's physical character and how it confuses our senses and makes rational thought difficult. Compton then dives into a long history of madness at sea, exploring how many age-old troubles are still echoed modern yacht races.

The Strange Last Voyage of Donald Crowhurst, Nicholas Tomalin and Ron Hall
(Hodder & Stoughton, 1970)
An utterly compelling account of Crowhurst's hoax journey and deteriorating state of mind, and a masterpiece of investigate journalism. The book contains lengthly passages from Crowhurst's conflicting logbooks, which often make for uncomfortable and poignant reading.

A Voyage for Madmen, Peter Nichols (Profile Books, 2002)
A vivid and riveting retelling of the journeys of all nine competitors in *The Sunday Times* Golden Globe race.

The highs and lows of commuting

Yorkshire's last miners | The New York skywalkers

Of all the journeys we make, none is so overlooked and treated with such disdain as the regular commute to work. Which is odd, considering that in many ways it's the most transformative journey of all. A commute isn't just about travelling between places, but moving between lives.

This is neatly illustrated by John Wemmick, the businesslike, stony-faced clerk in Dickens's *Great Expectations* (1861). At home, in his shoebox cottage in Walworth, Wemmick is a bright, warm-hearted eccentric, but as he walks into work, we read that, 'by degrees, Wemmick got dryer and harder … and his mouth tightened into a post-office.' By the time he arrives, the change is so absolute that the Wemmick of the office is 'only externally like the Wemmick of Walworth', and when he's asked to cast himself into his home persona for a moment, the clerk replies stiffly, 'Walworth is one place, and this office is another… My Walworth sentiments must be taken at Walworth; none but my official sentiments can be taken in this office.'

Most of us are Wemmicks to some extent. Our work self often dresses differently, uses expressions like 'quick win' and 'touch base' without shuddering, and walls off our personal life from our colleagues. People who bring their Walworth sentiments to work are unprofessional, while those who take their office selves home are workaholics. And it's the commute that keeps each twin in the right place.

Sometimes, though, it's not just the internal transformation but the journey itself that's remarkable, and therein lies the other fascinating thing about the commute. For commuters themselves, the journey is always ordinary, even when it would be utterly extraordinary to anyone else.

200

BEFORE KELLINGLEY COLLIERY closed on 18 December 2015, the 450 miners working at Britain's last deep coal mine began each shift with a journey straight out of a Jules Verne novel. Men with names like 'Funeral Face' bundled into a lift to descend about half a mile (800 m) below the surface of North Yorkshire, before filing on to a squat, flat-topped little train that would take them a further 4 miles (6.5 km) to the coal face. The work environment is beautifully evoked and commemorated in Wes Pollitt's documentary *The Last Miners* (2016).

As the wagons clacked through the tunnel towards what seemed like the centre of the Earth, the temperature edged above 30 degrees Celsius. Arriving at the coal face, the miners would peel off their coats and strip down to orange vests with fluorescent stripes that gleamed through the thick layer of black dust. They couldn't put cheese in their sandwiches because it would melt. To them, this would have been just a normal commute and the start of a regular day's work.

A hundred years earlier, in the same part of the world, Victorian guidebook writer Samuel Gordon accompanied the men of Upleatham ironstone mine to work. Proceeding in Indian file down the gloomy cavern, the workers had to stoop and inch their way for three-quarters of a mile (1.2 km) into the Cleveland ironstone seam. They soon became accustomed to the confined spaces and the dim light of the lamps as they moved further into the bowels of the Earth.

Kellingley Colliery was Britain's last deep coal mine. Men would descend half a mile (800 m) below the surface before filing on to a squat, flat-topped little train that would take them a further 4 miles (6.5 km) to the coal face.

As they descended, it wasn't just their perception of light and space that changed. The way sound travelled underground was alien, too. 'Every now and then,' wrote Gordon, 'an appalling detonation came, like a peal of thunder, rolling along the passages [and] reverberating through the vast labyrinth of galleries. It was a wild, weirdly scene, and so unearthly that we seemed to have found our way into the internal regions.'

Even the miners themselves took on an otherworldly aspect, with Gordon describing them variously as 'mischievous imps', 'dusky figures' and motionless marble statues with 'cold, vacant stares', bewildered by his intrusion into their subterranean world.

THOUGH SUCH journeys are a thing of the past in Britain, spare a thought for the miners in the Cerro Rico mountain of Potosí, Bolivia, known locally as 'the mountain that eats men'. One of the richest silver deposits in the world, it's been mined since the 1500s, and these days the mountain is wormed through with tunnels, where around 15,000 miners descend each day into some of the most nightmarish working conditions in the world. Gas, toxic dust and accidents mean life expectancy among the miners is barely above 40. Many of the miners are teenagers.

The Cerro Rico miners slither down into the darkness with bulging wads of coca leaves packed into their cheeks. Every now and again there is a low pop as someone sets off dynamite in a nearby tunnel, followed by a rush of warm air that blows their lamps out and plunges them into darkness. As they go deeper, they keep half an eye on the tell-tale flames of their carbide lamps. Too much flickering and they know something's wrong with the air.

Up where that air is fresh and open, the silver miners of Potosí are committed Catholics, but when they go to work deep in the asbestos-furred mines below ground, they leave the light of God behind them and consciously enter the realm of the Devil. The mines are dotted with poky little shrines containing crude statues of El Tío – a nightmarish horned figure festooned in coloured streamers. El Tío is king down here. It's customary to begin a shift by smoking an acrid clove cigarette with him (there's a blackened hole in his mouth to stick it in) and sharing a capful of over-proof grain alcohol. For reasons that are unclear, El Tío gets his share over his phallus, but the miners have to drink theirs – an experience not unlike huffing gasoline.

These offerings to El Tío are supposed to keep miners safe while they're on the Devil's turf, and you can see why they hedge their bets. For most of us, journeying to Hell and back is a rather melodramatic figure of speech, rather than an actual daily occurrence.

An engraving of miners in the Cerro Rico mountain of Potosí, 1596. The mountain is wormed with tunnels and boasts one of the richest silver deposits in the world.

Cerro Rico, the 'Wealthy Mountain' overshadows the streets of Potosí , Bolivia.

A miner opens the doors of a silver mine in Cerro Rico, Potosí, Bolivia.

The mines are dotted with poky little shrines containing crude statues of El Tío – a nightmarish horned figure festooned in coloured streamers. It's customary to begin a shift by smoking a clove cigarette with him and pouring a capful of over-proof grain alcohol over his phallus.

OF COURSE, there are two halves to a commute, and the second is every bit as transformative as the first. At the end of their shift, the miners of the Cerro Rico begin their journey back up towards light, life and God, just as the men of Kellingley and Upleatham did before them.

On emerging into the dazzling glare of daylight in 1869, Upleatham's miners were no longer the imps and golems of the underground. In the open air, the men of New Marske village (many of them economic migrants from London's East End) played cricket, sang lustily in chapel and attended winter lectures in the village reading room; their houses were remarkably 'clean and comfortable'. The strict divide between work and home life was not just preferred but actively enforced by management, partly stemming from an episode where a miner brought some dynamite home and accidentally blew up his house.

As for Kellingley's miners, their own passage back into the light involved a deep scrub in the showers (washing-up liquid was said to be good for its degreasing properties). They scoured off every speck of coal, then drove back to some of the most spotlessly well-kept homes ever seen. Clothes neat, gardens tidy, everything scrupulously clean – including the language, which was certainly not the case when the orange jackets were on. The contrast was extraordinary. Up in the daylight, the dust was only on the inside.

In their underground lives, the men of Kellingley looked different, sounded different and even had a different family. Their commute, that long ride on the paddy train, was a journey into a parallel life.

You change the way you are. You become a different person.
Kev, the shift overman, in The Last Miners *(dir. Wes Pollitt, 2016)*

LIKE A COMMUTE into the Earth's depths, the business of working at its higher points can be similarly precarious and surprising. Take, for instance, Clement Wragge, the meteorologist who spent a period of his career in the 1880s making daily ascents of Ben Nevis to take weather readings. Or how about the impossibly serene Ethiopian Coptic Christian priest Haileselassie Kahsay who scales a 820-foot (250-m) cliff each morning to get to his church. But perhaps the most iconic portrayal of working at height came courtesy of that student poster favourite, *Lunch atop a Skyscraper* (1932), a head-spinning photograph (possibly taken by Charles C. Ebbets) displaying a row of jaunty-looking workmen perched nonchalantly out on a beam on top of the Rockefeller Center.

Among such 'skywalkers' bolting together New York's cityscape, one particularly unusual band of long-distance commuters stands out. For more than a century, a disproportionate number of New York's ironworkers have been First Nations

Mohawks, schlepping all the way from the Kahnawake Reserve near Montreal in Canada to shin up girders and manhandle 8-ton beams up in the New York ether. Ironworking has been a tradition in Kahnawake since the late 1800s, when a self-confirming mythology sprang up about the Mohawks' head for heights.

They say Indians have a special knack for high jobs. I dunno. I guess a man takes the best thing that comes his way.
Harold McComber in High Steel *(dir. Don Owen, 1965)*

For a long time, the Mohawk skywalkers had their own little temporary community in Brooklyn – sending their families back home in the summers – but when Interstate 87 reached the Canadian border in the 1960s, it halved the journey time, signalling the beginning of a just-about-bearable commute. To this day, Sunday nights see ironworkers in Kahnawake piling in their trucks and making the 400-mile (640-km) drive down the Adirondack Highway to New York City, where they proceed to scale some of the tallest buildings on the planet and begin their working day. The local slang for this epic commute is 'booming out'.

In 2013 journalist Henry Gass recounted the journey to work of a modern-day ironworker called Pete Marquis. Marquis leaves Kahnawake around midnight, arriving

on-site in New York about seven hours later. 'After grabbing a coffee,' writes Gass, 'he spends the next eight hours hooking crane cables to the building's skeletal iron beams. By five o'clock, after more than 17 sleepless hours, he goes home and straight to bed.'

While the strange, weekly odyssey of 'booming out' isn't as popular as it once was, it hasn't died out quite yet. As work on One World Trade Center neared its final stages in 2012, it was estimated that around 10 per cent of the ironworkers regularly scaling North America's tallest building were Mohawk – a statistic given added poignancy by the fact that many of their fathers had worked on its predecessor.

> If someone were to see my portrait, I'd want them to know you're looking at someone who did their best to carry on the tradition of the Mohawks.
> *William Jacobs, in an interview with Melissa Cacciola, 'Skywalkers: The Legacy of the Mohawk Ironworker at the World Trade Center' (2015)*

For many Mohawks, the dangerous job in the eaves of the big city and the earthly anchor of the reservation are both parts of an ancestral identity, and that long drive through the night is the thread that holds them together. At the far end of that road lies a different world – a bucolic home life of neat clapboard houses and Tide-white washing, where the clanging of hammers and whine of heavy machinery gives way to the piping of birds and the buzz of bees among yellow blooms. Extraordinary as the career and the journey are, though, the Kahnawake Mohawks are essentially just commuters like the rest of us.

For the vast majority of commuters, the journey to work is an unremarkable chore, and there's something reassuring in the fact that everyone feels the same way about it, whether they're driving 400 miles (640 km) and ascending a skyscraper, or descending half a mile into the Earth and shuttling 4 miles (6 km) on the paddy train. But the real wonder of the commute is that it gives you a second identity to play with, neither more or less real than the one you've left behind at home. And, as people who've retired or been made redundant never cease to tell you, you'll miss it when it's gone. *JB*

SEEKER'S DIRECTORY

Documentaries
High Steel (dir. Don Owen, 1966)
Macho yet oddly sensitive documentary about Mohawk ironworkers in New York.

The Devil's Miner (dir. Kief Davidson and Richard Ladkani, 2005)
Haunting documentary following 14-year-old Basilio into the mines of the Cerro Rico.

The Last Miners (dir. Wes Pollitt, 2016)
Two-part documentary charting the final weeks of Kellingley Colliery, Britain's last deep coal mine.

Books
The Watering Places of Cleveland, Samuel Gordon (1869; reprinted Rigg, 1992)
Enthusiastic Victorian travel guide to north-east Yorkshire that gets sidetracked down an ironstone mine for ten pages or so.

Yorkshire People & Coal, Peter Tuffrey (Amberley Publishing, 2012)
A compilation of photos from the *Yorkshire Post* picture archives, charting the story of the Yorkshire coal industry from the 1960s pretty much to its demise.

Cleveland Ironstone Mines, David Currie and Stephen Sherlock (Printability Publishing Ltd, 1996)
A photographic guide to help industrial heritage geeks track down the crumbling remnants of 30-odd Victorian ironstone mines hidden away in North Yorkshire (including Upleatham).

An ironworker welding at a great height in Chicago.

Ironworkers going about their daily business building the Blue Cross Blue Shield Tower in Chicago.

The Merry Pranksters bus tour

Ken Kesey, Neal Cassady and Ken Babbs: countercultural
anti-heroes on America's last great road trip

It's all a myth now, anyway. Tell it however you want.
Ken Babbs, one of the original Merry Pranksters

To hell with facts! We need stories!
Ken Kesey

On 14 June 1964, 14 men and women boarded a converted 1939 International
Harvester school bus at a rural property in La Honda, California, and set out on a
road trip to New York City. Scrawled on the destination board over the bus's front
windscreen was a single, hand-lettered word: 'Further'.

Ken Kesey 1935–2001

The bus belonged to a 28-year-old Colorado-born writer, Ken Kesey, who, just a few
years before, had published a critically acclaimed, best-selling novel, *One Flew over
the Cuckoo's Nest*. Now his second novel, *Sometimes a Great Notion*, was about to be
released; he wanted to celebrate and promote it with a visit to the World's Fair in
New York. But what started out as a low-key, Kerouac-inspired idea of a cross-country
jaunt in the family station wagon soon morphed in something more ambitious: a road
movie to be shot on 16mm film with an expanded cast of friends and hangers-on,
and a narrative shaped not only by a meandering drift eastwards across the American
heartlands but also copious amounts of lysergic acid diethylamide, better known as
LSD or acid. Kesey ditched his station wagon and bought the school bus for $1,250.
   'I was too young to be a beatnik, and too old to be a hippie,' Kesey would tell an
interviewer, many years later. Long before anyone had heard of Haight-Ashbury in
San Francisco, Kesey was drawing a bohemian crowd to acid-stoked, sexually charged,

audiovisual 'happenings' at a log cabin surrounded by two-and-a-half forested acres that he had bought (with the profits from his first book) in La Honda, in the Santa Cruz Mountains south of the city. The regulars – writers, artists, musicians, groupies, actors, dancers, craftspeople, sound engineers, students and drug dealers – formed a loose gang. Kesey's best friend, Ken Babbs, dubbed them 'The Merry Pranksters'. 'I don't pick 'em,' Kesey said, 'I recognize 'em.'

Kesey wanted the bus to be a mobile extension of La Honda. The previous owner had already fitted it with bunks, water tanks, a toilet, a dinette and a makeshift galley. The Pranksters added an electrical generator, a sound system (with interior and exterior speakers, microphones, tape decks, instrument amplifiers and an early version of a synthesizer), an 'observation turret', and an exterior seating platform on a reinforced roof. A small, steel-framed deck was welded onto the rear of the chassis to house the generator and secure a motorcycle. The interior and exterior were painted in every imaginable colour, except the traditional school-bus yellow, forming patterns, symbols, celestial bodies, flowers, footprints, random words and phrases that were embellished or painted over several times.

Among the supplies loaded on board just before departure were musical instruments, three or four Bolex cameras, and approximately 12 miles (19 km) of 16mm colour film stock. There was also a large quantity of clinical-grade LSD (probably stolen from a local veteran's hospital), 500 Benzedrine tablets, and a shoebox

Among the supplies loaded on board were musical instruments, three or four Bolex cameras (*pictured*), and approximately 12 miles (19 km) of 16mm colour film stock. There was also a large quantity of LSD (probably stolen), 500 Benzedrine tablets, and a shoebox filled with pre-rolled joints.

filled with pre-rolled joints. No surprise then that elemental details of the trip itself have become a little hazy. It's not clear how some Pranksters came to be on the bus and why others – notably Kesey's wife, Faye – decided not to join them. Nor is it clear how the route to New York was plotted; both there and back, it stuck to the edges of the country, determined to avoid the centre, as if leaving open the option of a fast run for the border.

Neal Cassady 1926–1968

Nobody remembers how the hooligan-muse of the 1950s Beat Generation, Neal Cassady, the fabled Dean Moriarty of Jack Kerouac's *On the Road* (1957), ended up as the Prankster's wheelman. Kesey and his wife had met him for the first time a couple of years before, when they found him in their front yard in La Honda, 'smiling and rolling his shoulders this way and that and jerking his hands out to this side and the other side as if there's a different drummer somewhere … corked out of his gourd, in fact.' Or so Tom Wolfe wrote in *The Electric Kool-Air Acid Test* a decade later. The novelist Robert Stone described Cassady as 'the world's greatest driver, who could roll a joint while backing a 1937 Packard onto the lip of the Grand Canyon', and when he turned up at La Honda again, pretty much at the last minute, he replaced Roy Sebern in the driver's seat. The artist who had painted much of the bus and dubbed it 'Furthur' (at least, until Kesey corrected the spelling) decided to remain behind.

Top left The Pranksters painted the bus in psychedelic colours, forming patterns, symbols, celestial bodies, flowers, footprints, random words and phrases that were embellished or painted over several times.

Above 1965 Acid Test Flyer. The Acid Tests were a series of parties held by Ken Kesey in the San Francisco Bay Area during the mid-1960s, focused entirely on the use and advocacy of, the psychedelic drug LSD.

Left Neal Cassady (*left*) with fellow beatnik Jack Kerouac.

'Further' rattled southwards to Los Angeles and beyond, to the heart of John Wayne-style Southern Californian conservatism, Orange County.

There were doubts that the quarter-of-a-century-old bus would make it out of La Honda, let alone across the country. On the morning of departure, 'Further' rolled down Kesey's driveway, with the sound system blaring Ray Charles's 'Hit the Road, Jack' – and ran out of gas. Even with a full tank, its ageing, under-serviced engine and drive-train forced so many stops that it took 24 hours to cover the first 40 miles (64 km).

WHEN THE PRANKSTERS finally arrived in the city of San José, one of the few women aboard, a 38-year-old dancer named Chloe Scott decided to get off the bus. Cathryn (Cathy) Marie Casamo, a Northwestern University drama major and single mother, was enlisted to take her place, not only on the bus but in the chaotic, unscripted movie Kesey began shooting as 'Further' rattled southwards to Los Angeles and beyond, to the heart of John Wayne-style Southern Californian conservatism,

Orange County. After a two-day layover close to the coast, at the San Juan Capistrano home of Prankster Ken Babbs – who, just a year before, had been serving as a marine officer with one of the first US 'advisory' units in Vietnam – the Pranksters headed inland, towards the desert.

From the outset, the Pranksters were on a mission. Kesey imagined their course eastwards as deliberately contrarian, stemming the tide of an historic east–west flow of European settlement across the country. Four and a half decades before the idea (and the word) became a debased cliché in Silicon Valley, Kesey wanted 'to break through conformist thought and ultimately forge a reconfiguration of American society', capturing average folk's attention with random acts of outlandish performance art and whenever possible expanding their consciousness with hits of still-legal hallucinogens.

Kesey's very American impulse to take to the road in search of 'another place' – physical, emotional, spiritual, it didn't much matter which – translated neatly as a metaphor for the chemically induced, psycho-spiritual 'trip' into an interior self that LSD provided. Kesey and the rest of the Pranksters were 'tripping' in every sense. And they were determined to share this with the rest of the country.

'Taking acid led to an expansion of consciousness and a way of seeing things through new eyes, delighting in the world the way a child does,' Ken Babbs explained later. 'It was an experience that was bigger than music, bigger than poetry or plays or novels … It's about everything happening outside of time, in the past, present and future all at once.'

Kesey's interest in hallucinogens dated to 1959, when he was working as a night aide at the Menlo Park Veterans' Hospital. Some of the CIA's MKUltra-sponsored studies on hallucinogenic drugs (including LSD, psilocybin mescaline, cocaine and DMT) were being undertaken at the hospital and Kesey volunteered to be a test subject. Later, he stole doses of LSD from the hospital – the drug itself was legal in California until 1966 – and conducted experiments of his own within a bohemian community of Stanford academics in Palo Alto, wreaking all kinds of havoc.

Proto-hippies, outsiders and anti-heroes, Kesey and the Pranksters were modelling with unlikely precision the aesthetic and attitudinal foundations not only of 'flower power' but a youth counterculture that, within just a couple of years, would corrode the accepted norms and values of the suburban middle-American Dream.

Still, none of this had occurred to anybody in the early summer of 1964, as 'Further' nosed deeper into the dusty back country of the Southwest, urged onwards

Outside the one-horse town of Wikieup, Arizona, the Pranksters took a detour to go skinny-dipping. 'Further' got bogged in soft, alluvial sand. While some set off to find a tow, others turned the long wait into an 'acid test'.

by Neal Cassady's relentless, carnival carney-like, streams-of-consciousness shtick. The Pranksters found themselves welcomed in some small towns as if they were a travelling circus. They would give the locals impromptu performances of poetry and music in the middle of the main street, using the bus's rooftop as a stage. And they would clown for the kids, who would run alongside the bus, waving, laughing, when the time came for 'Further' to continue on its way.

The Prankster ethos was gentle, playful and non-confrontational. Beneath their colourful face-paint, the women had an anodyne, all-American, 'white bread' kind of prettiness – wide-eyed and giggling like homecoming queens, maybe because they were always stoned; the men were mainly short-haired and clean-cut, outdoorsy farm boys and veterans, with just a few mop-topped, Californian college types, who, when they weren't bare-chested, wore variations of the national colours – red, white and blue – in stripes on their T-shirts and shirts (one of Kesey's ideas). No whiff of protest, sedition or subversion – none of them looked like hippies.

'We weren't anti-American,' Babbs recalled. 'We always tried to embody the great American ideal, which is freedom: the freedom to do what you want with your own body, and to do what you want with your own lives. We were pranksters, but there was no cruelty or malice to our work, and we never made anyone the butt of our pranks…'

There was, however, little diversity among the Pranksters: no blacks, no Hispanics, no Native Americans. And the men outnumbered the women by nearly five to one.

Outside the one-horse town of Wikieup, Arizona, the Pranksters took a detour to

When the bus reached Phoenix, Cassady convinced his stoned compadres to paint 'A Vote for Barry is a Vote for FUN!' above the bus's windows. He then drove slowly, in reverse, through the city's centre.

the Big Sandy River – in reality, an intermittent desert stream – to go skinny-dipping. 'Further' got bogged in the soft, alluvial sand. While a couple of the Pranksters set off to find a tractor to tow the bus out, the remainder turned the long wait under the desert sun into an 'acid test'. When the bus reached Phoenix later that day, Cassady convinced his stoned compadres to paint 'A Vote for Barry is a Vote for FUN!' above the bus's windows on one side. He then drove slowly, in reverse, through the city's centre, past the campaign headquarters for US Presidential candidate Barry Goldwater.

Cathy Casamo dropped a little too much acid during the riverside party in Wikieup, and for most of the long, hot, night-time drive between Phoenix and Houston, she insisted on dancing naked on the cargo deck at the rear of the bus; long-haul truckers saluted her with blasts from their air-horns.

Cathy earned one of the Pranksters' best-remembered (albeit most prosaic) nicknames – Stark Naked – and she was still naked and tripping the next morning when 'Further' pulled up outside the Houston home of the best-selling author Larry McMurtry. 'Ken called and said they were coming to see me; little did I know that the breeze of the future was about to blow through my quiet street,' McMurtry wrote in a brief memoir, 'Stark Gets off the Bus'.

> There it came, the bus whose motto was Further ... My son James, aged two, was sitting in the yard in his diapers when the bus stopped and a naked lady ran out and grabbed him. It was Stark Naked (later shortened to Stark), who, being temporarily of a disordered mind, mistook him for her own little girl. James, in diapers, had no objection to naked people, and the neighbours, most of them staid Republicans, took this event in their stride ...
> Larry McMurtry, 'Stark Gets off the Bus' (Spit in the Ocean, *issue 7, 2003*)

Cathy went missing that night. The Pranksters spent 24 hours searching the city for her. She was found by the police, who confined her to a holding cell in downtown Houston: 'She has no I.D., no shoes, and she bit the arresting officer,' the desk sergeant told McMurty, when he finally tracked her down. 'Do you know if she's on anything?' But before she could be bailed, the police transferred her to a public asylum on the outskirts of Houston, 'a massive, grey, hospital building out of a Batman comic book' (McMurtry, again), for observation. The Pranksters decided to push on without her.

'If you're not on the bus, you're off the bus.' It became an oft-repeated catch-phrase of mid-1960s counterculture – but it was originally just Kesey's caveat to a bus-load of stoned, unruly Pranksters.

MAIS LAISSEZ LES bons temps rouler! Wanting to show the Pranksters a better time, Neal Cassady steered them to New Orleans, and after a night of partying in the French

Wanting to show the Pranksters a good time, Neal Cassady steered them to New Orleans for a night of partying in the French Quarter followed by swimming in Lake Pontchartrain.

Quarter, they found their way to a beach on the shores of Lake Pontchartrain to go swimming. The trouble was, Louisiana in the 1960s was a tense, racially segregated state, and the beach was one of just a few reserved for blacks. For the blacks there, the Pranksters presence was an unwanted intrusion, an exertion of resented white privilege, although the Pranksters were too stoned to realize it. When they did, Kesey recalled, 'I don't think a word was said. We all just got back on the bus and left.'

It says something about the antic novelty of the Pranksters, in those early years of the 1960s, that, although they had plenty of run-ins with law enforcement on the trip, none resulted in any of them being busted – not even Stark Naked, who was eventually released into the care of a boyfriend – despite the bus's cargo of illicit dope and speed. A year later, Kesey would go on the run and eventually face jail time for possession and suspicion of dealing, but in that still innocent summer of 1964, a random stop by the highway patrol or a curious hick sheriff resulted in little more than a request for a licence and identification, a few questions, a bit of head-scratching, and maybe a twitchy caution that the Pranksters should think about being out of their jurisdiction by sundown.

From New Orleans, there was a short run along the Gulf Coast, through Gulfport and Biloxi, to Pensacola, in Florida, to visit a buddy of Ken Babbs, before 'Further' turned northwards for New York City. And apart from leaving behind Ken Babbs's younger brother, John, after a toilet stop in South Carolina – he managed to hitch a

ride and catch up with them – the drive to New York was relatively uneventful.

A suspicion lingers that the Pranksters' arrival in New York, on 29 June, was something of an anti-climax, a let-down or, at least, less than Kesey had hoped. As soon as the Pranksters hit 'Madhatten', as they called it, Kesey phoned his literary agent, Sterling Lord, and told him, 'The city just rolled over on its back and purred.'

The Pranksters took over an apartment on Madison Avenue, between 89th and 90th, that 'first-off-the-bus' Chloe Scott had located for them – 'Further' was parked in front of the 90th Street Pharmacy, just across the street – kicking off what would become a week-long party. Among the first visitors was the author Robert Stone, an old friend of Kesey's from Stanford University, who wrote of their long friendships in a 2007 memoir, *Prime Green*: 'He really seemed capable of making anything happen. We sat and smoked, and Possibility came down on us.'

Top of Kesey's 'Madhatten' wish list was meeting the legendary chronicler of the Beat Generation, Jack Kerouac. Kesey and his friends imagined themselves as the natural successors of the freewheeling, poetic and spiritually questing Beats, and a meeting with Jack was seen, somehow, as an opportunity to gain his imprimatur.

It wasn't to be.

Kerouac's former lover Neal Cassady phoned the poet Allen Ginsberg, and together with Allen's lover and fellow-poet, Peter Orlovsky, and Peter's brother, Julius – who had just been released from a 14-year confinement in a mental institution – they organized to drive to Northport, Long Island, to pick up Jack Kerouac. When they all arrived at the Madison Avenue apartment, the Pranksters were so cranked up – the apartment filled with 'spontaneous combustion musical and verbal make-believe shenanigans', as Ken Babbs described it – the world-weary, alcoholic, 42-year-old Kerouac was driven to an armchair in the corner of the room, where he remained, aloof and unwelcoming. When the Pranksters draped a small American flag over his shoulders, 'he took it off, folded it neatly, and placed it on the arm of the couch'. Kerouac left without conversing with Kesey after just an hour.

The Pranksters' outing to the New York World's Fair was also a bust. Alex Gibney – the American film-maker who, 47 years later, would edit 100 hours of 16mm film footage and sound captured on the bus into the coherent, watchable, 2012 documentary *The Magic Trip* – told an interviewer, 'They thought they were going to hang out in a vision of the future, but it turned out the World's Fair was actually a vision of the past. The future was them, the future was now, the future was right there on the bus.'

Any doubt that the road trip had taken a wrong turn was erased when the Pranksters, accompanied by Allen Ginsberg, set off upstate to meet Timothy Leary, the infamous psychologist and public proselytizer for the spiritual potential of hallucinogens. Together with Richard Alpert, who would become known as Ram

The Pranksters paid a visit to New York World's Fair, expecting to hang out in a vision of the future.

A statue of famous Oregon author Ken Kesey reading to children in the middle of downtown Eugene.

FURTHER

YES, This is Ken Kesey and the Merry Pranksters "Magic Bus"

This is not a replica, it is not named "Further 2", it is the second bus, the first died in the 60's. This bus traveled many miles with Ken and the Pranksters, to NY, Canada, and the United Kingdom. Both buses are named Further and Furthur, depending on our mood. The first bus was a 1939 International, this is a 1947. The older Further is in storage at the Kesey farm waiting to be restored for museum visits and special occasions. Please do not climb on the bus. Please take as many pictures as you want...she likes that!

The original 'Further' sits to pasture on the Kesey farmstead in rural Oregon, waiting for funding to be refurbished.

Dass, Leary had set up the International Foundation for Internal Freedom (aka IFIF) at Millbrook – a 2,500-acre (1,000-ha) estate near Poughkeepsie, New York, owned by heirs to the Mellon fortune. (This was after their less-than-rigorous studies on the therapeutic possibilities of psychedelic drugs had resulted in both men being dismissed from Harvard University.)

The Pranksters were not exactly welcomed with open arms. Their amplified singing and the coloured smoke grenades they tossed from the rooftop of the bus as it made its way up Millbrook's driveway might have had something to do with it. Leary, who was said to be tripping on acid, hid out. It was left to Richard Alpert to greet them. Only later did Leary surface long enough to say hello to Cassidy – Allen Ginsberg snapped a photo of both of them together in the bus – but he snubbed Kesey and the rest of the Pranksters, leaving them to cool their heels on the mansion's wide, bow-fronted, Colonial verandah.

Neal Cassady stepped off the bus and disappeared after the visit to Millbrook, and without his amphetamine-amped vibe, the long drive home to California, skirting the northern border with Canada this time, occasionally straying over it, was something of an anti-climax. The cast of Pranksters changed: new people climbed aboard, others stepped off; once stable emotional relationships became mutable and there were experiments with what was later touted as 'free love'. It didn't work all that well for everybody.

When the bus finally returned to La Honda, Kesey urged the Pranksters to burn their 'bus clothes' on the lawn in front of his home. 'I was done with it,' he said. 'I wanted to get back to business. I had books to write, kids to raise. But it wouldn't die. People just kept coming round.'

IN MANY WAYS, the transcontinental road trip was just the beginning for Kesey and the Pranksters: they had, quite literally, sown the seeds of not only a psychedelic, pop cultural revolution but a seismic social shift that amplified with the growing economic power of youth. Within a year, a Grateful Dead sound engineer turned chemist, Owsley Stanley III, would manufacture industrial amounts of LSD for sale to the Pranksters and everyone else in the USA who wanted it; within three years Timothy Leary would instruct a crowd of 30,000 at an event called Human Be-In, in San Francisco's Golden Gate Park, to 'Turn on, tune in, drop out'. The city's much-vaunted Summer of Love, in 1967, when 100,000 young hippies from all over the USA made their way to Haight-Ashbury to hang out and get stoned, was the culmination of a journey that began when Ken Kesey and the Pranksters first set out across America from La Honda, three years before.

Kesey's 'acid tests' became a mainstay of California's countercultural scene, with screenings of fragments of Kesey's film footage, light shows, performances by the Grateful Dead and, essentially, communal experiences of LSD – until 1966, when

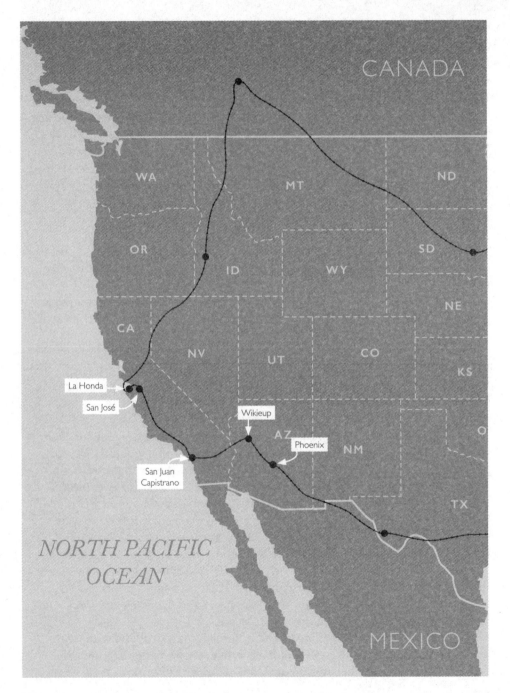

La Honda

San José

Wikieup

Phoenix

San Juan
Capistrano

NORTH PACIFIC
OCEAN

CANADA

WA

MT

ND

OR

ID

SD

WY

NE

CA

NV

UT

CO

KS

AZ

NM

O

TX

MEXICO

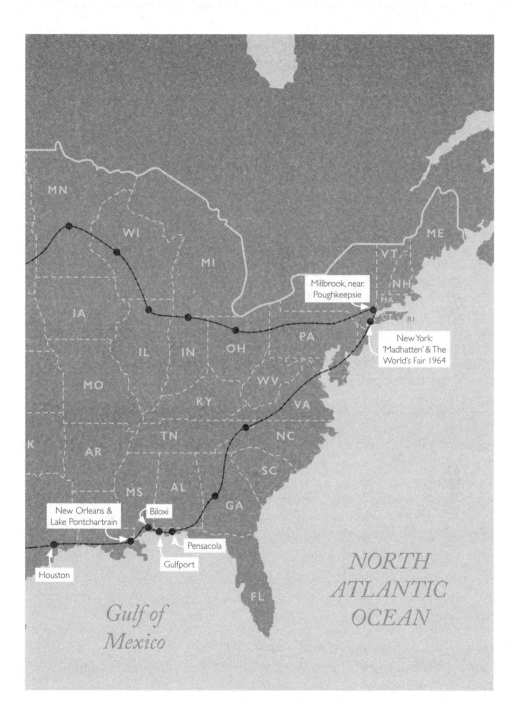

Millbrook, near.
Poughkeepsie

MN

WI

MI

ME

VT

NH

MA

CT

RI

New York:
'Madhatten' & The
World's Fair 1964

IA

IL

IN

OH

PA

MO

WV

KY

VA

K

AR

TN

NC

MS

AL

SC

GA

New Orleans &
Lake Pontchartrain

Biloxi

Pensacola

Gulfport

Houston

FL

NORTH
ATLANTIC
OCEAN

Gulf of
Mexico

California and Nevada became the first states to prohibit the manufacture, sale and possession of LSD (the US Congress passed the Staggers–Dodd Act, criminalizing the recreational use of LSD-25 in all states, in October 1968). Inevitably, Kesey himself fell foul of the law. In April 1965 a team of local sheriff's deputies led by a federal DEA agent raided Kesey's home in La Honda and arrested him and 13 others for marijuana possession. 'I don't like to divide the world into "them" and "us" but people here don't seem to be able to leave us alone,' Kesey told a reporter.

The Prankster story descended into farce: Kesey staged a fake suicide, then went on the run aboard 'Further' with his family and the Pranksters. They made it across the border into Mexico, where they stayed for eight months, drifting from Puerto Vallarta to Mazatlán to the dead-end jungle port of Manzanillo, until homesickness drove Kesey home; in January 1966 he turned himself in and was sentenced to six months in the San Mateo County jail, in Redwood City.

By the end of 1968, less than a year after the Summer of Love, all innocence was lost. Neal Cassady was found dying of drug-induced renal failure alongside a railway track outside San Miguel de Allende in Mexico; Jack Kerouac would die of alcoholism the following year; Martin Luther King was assassinated in Memphis, and a few months later, in Washington, DC, so was Robert Kennedy; Richard Nixon was elected president; America committed tens of thousands young American lives to an unwinnable war in Vietnam War; the country was divided by increasingly bloody protests. The USA was no place for pranks anymore, merry or otherwise. *CCO'H*

SEEKER'S DIRECTORY

Film
Magic Trip: Ken Kesey's Search for a Kool Place (dir. Alex Gibney and Alison Ellwood, 2011)
A freewheeling portrait of Ken Kesey and the Merry Pranksters' road trip across the USA, created from the Prankster's original 16mm footage, interspersed with contemporary interviews with the surviving members.

Books
The Electric Kool-Aid Acid Test, Tom Wolfe (Farrar Straus Giroux, 1968)
An unflinching portrait of Ken Kesey, the Pranksters, LSD and the latter half of 1960s. A pioneering work of New Journalism.

The Further Enquiry, Ken Kesey (Viking, 1990)
Originally intended as a film script, this book contains hundreds of photographs and transcripts of key episodes in Kesey's own re-examination of the 1964 road trip.

On the Bus: The Complete Guide to the Legendary Trip of Ken Kesey and the Merry Pranksters and the Birth of Counterculture, Paul Perry (Running Press, 1997)
An attempt to capture the energy of the 1964 legendary trip with candid photos, interviews with participants and witnesses, a hybrid essay/fantasy by prankster Ken Babbs and extracts from Tom Wolfe's account in *The Electric Kool-Aid Acid Test*.

Collected Letters 1944-1967, Neal Cassady, ed. David Moore (Penguin Books, 2005)
A collection of more than two hundred letters written by the driver of the psychedelic bus, to Jack Kerouac, Allen Ginsberg, John Clellon Holmes and other Beat generation luminaries.

For years, 'Further' was relegated to a swamp on Kesey's family farm, before Ken's son Zane hitched up a tractor and towed it out so it could await restoration.

About the authors

DAVID BRAMWELL

David is a regular contributor to BBC Radio 3 and Radio 4. He has made programmes on subjects ranging from Ivor Cutler to time travel and been a guest on *The Museum of Curiosity*, *The Danny Baker Show* and *The Verb*. In 2011 he won a Sony Silver Award for 'Best Feature' for his work on Radio 3's *The Haunted Moustache*. As a podcaster he co-presents the fortnightly *Odditorium* and presents and produces *Waterfront* on behalf of the Canal & River Trust.

He is also the creator of the best-selling *Cheeky Guides* series and author of two travel memoirs, *The No9 Bus to Utopia* ('Packed with gags, wisdom and pathos' Tom Hodgkinson) and *The Haunted Moustache* ('Neurologically, this will light you up like a Christmas tree' Alan Moore).

As a performer David is singer in the band Oddfellow's Casino, has toured several award-winning shows and enjoys giving entertaining lectures on topics ranging from ghost villages to occultism. He is at his happiest performing in the back room of a pub, provided at least five people show up, that is.

'A remarkable storyteller.' (*Radio Times*)

drbramwell.com
@drbramwell

JO TINSLEY

A devotee to slow and thoughtful journalism, Jo is proud to be part of a growing subculture of independent publishers. She is the founder of *Ernest Journal*, a magazine for the curious and adventurous that encourages readers to slow down and appreciate simple pleasures while rekindling a thirst for knowledge and exploration.

She is also the editor of *Waterfront*, a magazine for Friends of the Canal & River Trust, which satisfies her healthy inclination towards Victorian invention and lets her geek out over river etymology and ox-bow lakes. She also curates talks and immersive experiences on the theme of water and landscape for festivals.

As well as co-authoring *The Odditorium* and *The Mysterium*, Jo contributed to *Wild Guide: Devon, Cornwall and South West* (2013), writes for *Lonely Planet, Countryfile, Sawdays, The Simple Things, The Guardian* and *The Independent* and has spoken about independent publishing for a Guardian Masterclass and various other events.

A lido lover and sea swimmer, Jo is never happier than when immersed in water or when rambling over northern moorlands and exploring Britain's peculiar corners.

slowjo.co.uk
@SlowJoTinsley

The Odysseum team

ernest.

Ernest is a journal for enquiring minds. It's made for those who value surprising and meandering journeys, fuelled by curiosity rather than adrenaline and guided by chance encounters. It is a repository for wild ideas, curious artefacts and genuine oddities, replete with tales of pioneers, invention and human obsession.

Ernest is founded on the principles of slow journalism. We value honesty, integrity and down-to-earth storytelling – and a good, long read every now and then.

ernestjournal.co.uk

'It's hard to describe the excitement I felt when I first held a copy of *Ernest Journal*. It was as though someone had reached into the deepest recesses of my mind and turned its muddled lumber into an exquisite object. It was like that moment when you meet someone and know you'll be friends for life. I have to force myself to read it slowly. Every word, every beautiful illustration feels charged with meaning and makes me want to pull on my boots and wander off into the unknown.'
John Mitchinson, *QI*

'*Ernest Journal* is ridiculously beautiful and almost too wonderful to read. Getting the latest edition is like holding the new album from your favourite band before you've played it.'
Wolfgang Wild, *Retronaut*

Launch of the Year, Digital Magazine Awards (2014)
Shortlisted for Magpile's Best New Magazine (2014)

The *Odditorium* podcast, which features episodes on people covered in *The Odditorium: The tricksters, eccentrics, deviants and inventors whose obsessions changed the world* (Hodder & Stoughton, 2016), is a portal into the fringes of culture: its mavericks and pranksters, adventurers and occultists, artists, comics, eroticists and even the odd chef. Each episode features a guest speaker recorded before a live audience. It is ably hosted by author David Bramwell and comic actor Dave Mounfield (BBC Radio 4's *Count Arthur Strong's Radio Show*), who frame the topic with their mixture of humour, insight, silliness and an obsession with biscuits. The show is produced by Andrew Mailing and double Sony Award-winner Lance Dann, whose sound design adds an extra layer of wit and spice to the mix. The podcast broke into iTunes' top ten Arts and Culture list, has featured in *The Guardian's* 'Top 50 Essential Podcasts' and continues to tour with live events at festivals.

Why does a dolphin's vagina corkscrew? What is the best song to commit suicide to? Why is a hanged man's severed hand so valuable? What is the origin of the rudest word in English? Why are we so obsessed with big willies? Subscribe to the podcast and you will find out all the answers you need, and a few you don't.

Subscribe to the *Odditorium* podcast on iTunes, Stitcher or your favourite podcatcher, oddpodcast.com

'A taste for genius matched by eccentricity'
Bella Todd, *The Guardian*

Contributors

JOLY BRAIME

Joly has written on subjects as diverse as Viking dialect, the effective use of chloroform, hiking routes in the Dolomites and *Fifty Shades of Grey*. He lives in North Yorkshire with a tortoise and a poodle, and enjoys tramping the moors and filling his coal shed with home brew. **jolybraime.co.uk**

C. C. O'HANLON

C. C. O'Hanlon is a relentless traveller and occasional diarist. He has also been a musician, seaman, stand-over man, smuggler, gambler, photographer, web entrepreneur, and government adviser. His writing has been published widely and included in several anthologies and 'best of ... collections. Born in Sydney and raised nearly everywhere else, he has lived for the past few years in Berlin. **@ccohanlon**

GUY LOCHHEAD

Guy is a writer and weightlifting coach in Easton, Bristol. In 2016 he founded Bristol Co-operative Gym (bristolcooperativegym.org) as an inclusive, body-positive training space that's run by its members. It is the first co-operatively run gym in the UK. In his spare time, he enjoys writing and researching for *Ernest Journal*. **guylochhead.com**

DAVE MOUNFIELD

David is an actor, writer and presenter, best known for his roles as Geoffrey, Gerry and Jack in the Sony Gold Award-winning *Count Arthur Strong's Radio Show* for Radio 4 and various characters in Sky Atlantic's *This Is Jinsy* and Channel 4's *Tripped*. He has co-authored *The Cheeky Guide to Student Life*, *The Cheeky Guide to Love* and the multi-award-winning play 'Follow Me'. He co-presents *The Odditorium* Podcast. **@Mounders**

JEN ROWE

Jen writes short fiction with a speculative edge, with which she's had a modicum of success. She also writes for the stage, including poetry, short plays and her recent solo show '*Tiptree*' – exploring the life of American science fiction writer Alice Sheldon. As well as writing, Jen is an actor and voiceover artist. She regularly performs – and runs workshops – with improvisation companies themaydays.com, Impromptu Shakespeare and other theatrical institutions. **jennyrowe.co.uk**

DIXE WILLS

Dixe is an author, travel writer and soya connoisseur. His books include *Tiny Islands*, *Tiny Stations* and *Tiny Britain*, while his travel writing appears mainly in the notoriously liberal-leftie organ *The Guardian*, along with a selection of magazines of no particular political persuasion. His home largely comprises prisoner-of-war escape books. **dixewills.com**

Acknowledgements

The authors would like to extend thanks to: Ross Gurney-Randall, Stilly, Thryza Segal, Carrie Reichardt, Andrew Kötting, Nic Compton, Jak Hutchcraft.

With particular thanks to our publishing team at Hodder & Stoughton, Jonathan Shipley, Iain Campbell, Christina Wood and Robert Tuesley Anderson, as well as Lance Dann, Andrew Mailing and Dave Mounfield from *Odditorium* podcast.

Finally, to our diligent and talented researchers Guy Lochhead and Matthew Iredale, to Mark Blackmore for his original story 'Hunter and the Giant' in Issue 2, and to all of the *Ernest Journal* team for working tirelessly to design and edit *The Odysseum* – thank you!

PHOTO CREDITS

JOURNEYS OF CONFINEMENT Bauamt Süd, Einofski (p. 11); United States Army Signal Corps photographer / Harvard Law School Library, Harvard University (p. 12); Xavier de Maistre / Guillaume (p. 18).

X MARKS THE SPOT Tigerfry (p. 25); flickr/Les Chatfield (p. 33).

ATMOSPHERIC JOURNEYS flickr / Brandon Walts / Omnibus (p. 37); Deutsches US Navy National Museum of Naval Aviation (p.39); pexels.com (p. 40); pixabay.com (p. 42); Alamy / Everett Collection Historical (p. 44). Wikimedia / Das Matejko Buch / Theo Matejko (p. 45); NOAA Ship Collection / Archival Photography by Steve Nicklas, NOS, NGS (p. 46)

TOTEMIC JOURNEYS NASA / Neil A. Armstrong (p. 49); NASA (p. 50); Getty Images / Peter Macdiarmid / Staff (p. 53); John Muir Trust (p. 54); Alamy / Photo 12 (pp. 62, 63); Wikimedia / Dr. Eugen Lehle (p. 64).

STRANGE CARGO Alamy / Everett Collection Inc (p. 67); flickr/clipperarctic (p. 74).

THE ROAD TO EN-DOR C.W. HILL, Lt. R.A.F / Tony Craven Walker & Hilary Bevan Jones (pp. 77, 78, 81, 84); Annan / Tony Craven Walker & Hilary Bevan Jones (p. 82); Savony / Tony Craven Walker & Hilary Bevan Jones (p. 83); Talha Bey / Tony Craven Walker & Hilary Bevan Jones (p. 87).

DETOURS OF THE DEAD flickr / jennybento (p. 93); flickr / cp_thornton (p. 94); flickr / Ron (p. 94); David Bramwell (p. 96); Carrie Reichardt (pp. 97, 99, 100); Museo del Bicentenario (p. 105); Deensel (p. 109); Jimmy Harris (p. 109).

VOYAGE TO THE CENTRE OF THE EARTH Wellcome Collection (p. 103); Wikimedia / Numa Ayrinhac (1881–1951) / Museo Casa Rosada (p. 128).

JOURNEYS OF LOVE AND LOSS Wikimedia / Abhas Kumar Kheti (p. 127); Sten-M. Rosenlund / REX / Shutterstock (p. 128); Wikimedia / Nicolas Perrault III (p. 131); British Library / Charles Hannan (p. 133); flickr / Wikimedia / Nicolas Perrault III (p. 131); British Library / Charles Hannan (p. 133); flickr / Andrew Russeth / Marina Abramovic / MOMA (p. 134).

THE FINAL FIX Christiaan Tonnis (p. 137); Wikimedia / Terpsichore (p. 138); flickr / Apollo (p. 139); Wikimedia / Harvard University (p. 141); Wikimedia / Boston Public Library / Rinehart, Frank. A (p. 141); Wikimedia / National Anthropological Collection / unbekannt 1892 (p. 141); Wikimedia / panza.rayada (p. 142); Wikimedia / Jialiang Gao, www.peace-on-earth.org (p. 145); Wikimedia / Alan Rockefeller (p. 146); Wikimedia / Mark Goff (pp. 150, 151); Wikimedia / Jon Hanna (p. 152).

THE DADAIST JOURNEYMAN flickr / Dave Smith (p. 165); Andrew Kötting (pp. 166, 168, 169, 173); flickr / David Holt (p. 167); Wikimedia / JackyR (p. 167).

BECALMED: TALES OF ISOLATION AT SEA NOAA Central Library Historical Collections (p. 175); Alamy / Keystone Pictures USA (pp. 176, 184); pixabay.com (p. 179); Wikimedia / Barry Lewis (p. 187); Wikimedia / Tinmothian (p. 188); Wikimedia / Pietbarber (p. 194); Wikimedia / Image courtesy of Islands in the Sea 2002, NOAA/OER (p. 194); Wikimedia / Gothick (p. 196); flickr / Lee Shoal (p. 197).

THE HIGHS AND LOWS OF COMMUTING flickr / Chris Sampson (p. 201); Library of Congress / Lewis Wicks Hine (p. 202); Wikimedia / Historia Americae sive Novi Orbis / Theodor de Bry (p. 203);
Wikimedia / Mhwater at Dutch Wikipedia (p. 204); Wikimedia / Marco Ebreo (p. 204); flickr / Andy Young (p. 204); flickr / Petr Meissner (p. 206); Wikimedia / Professor Jean-Claude Latombe (p. 207); flickr / Timo Goodrich (p. 209).

THE MERRY PRANKSTER TOUR BUS Wikimedia / Jmabel (p. 211, 222); Wikimedia / Tieum512 (p. 212); Wikimedia / Paul Foster / Ken Kesey (p. 213); Wikimedia / FoundSF (p. 213);
Wikimedia / Rcarlberg (pp. 213, 227); Wikimedia / Orange County Archives (p. 214, 215); Wikimedia / Chris English (p. 216); goodfreephotos.com (p. 217); Wikimedia / Post Card Specialties, New Orleans, LA (p. 219); flickr / The Tichnor Brothers Collection / Boston Public Library, Print Department (p. 220);
Wikimedia / Anthony Conti; scanned and published by PLCjr from Richmond, VA, USA (p. 221);
Pete Helzer / sculptor / photographer (p. 222).

The Odditorium (2016)

The Odditorium: The tricksters, eccentrics, deviants and inventors whose obsessions changed the world is a playful retelling of history, told not through the lens of its victors, but through the fascinating stories of a wealth of individuals who carved their own path in life.

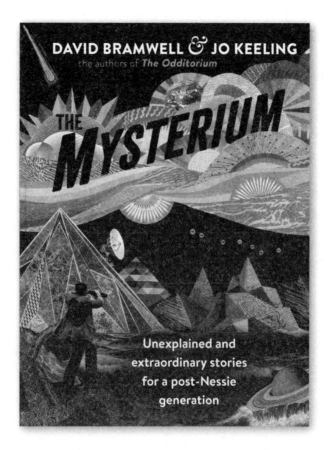

The Mysterium (2017)

Drawing on contemporary folklore, unsolved mysteries and unsettling oddities from the dark corners of the Internet, *The Mysterium: Unexplained and extraordinary stories for a post-Nessie generation* delves into some of the strangest and most enduring stories of our modern age.

The Brewer's Dictionary of Phrase & Fable, 19th Edition

Much loved for its wit and wisdom since 1870, when Dr E. Cobham Brewer published his landmark dictionary, the Brewer's range of books provides a scenic route to knowledge, taking you on a captivating adventure through everything you never knew you wanted to know. Exuberantly eclectic and cheerfully unpredictable, a Brewer's book is irresistible to anyone who relishes a meander through the more unusual byways of life.

For more information about titles available
from Chambers, please visit
www.chambers.co.uk